ZOHAR

ZOHAR
THE BOOK OF SPLENDOR

SELECTED AND EDITED BY
GERSHOM SCHOLEM

SCHOCKEN BOOKS · NEW YORK

First SCHOCKEN PAPERBACK *edition 1963*

15 14 13 12 11   80 81 82 83

CONTENTS

Contents

Historical Setting of the Zohar

The book of Zohar, the most important literary work of
the Kabbalah, lies before us in some measure inaccessible
and silent, as befits a work of secret wisdom. Whether because of this, or in spite of it, among the great literary
products of our medieval writings, however much clearer
and more familiar than the Zohar many of them seem to
us, not one has had an even approximately similar influence or a similar success. To have determined the forma-
tion and development over a long period of time of the
religious convictions of the widest circles in Judaism, and
particularly of those most sensitive to religion, and, what
is more, to have succeeded in establishing itself for three
centuries, from about 1500 to 1800, as a source of doctrine
and revelation equal in authority to the Bible and Talmud,
and of the same canonical rank—this is a prerogative that
can be claimed by no other work of Jewish literature. This
radiant power did not, to be sure, emanate at the very beginning from "The Book of Radiance" or, as we usually
render the title in English, "The Book of Splendor." Maimonides' "Guide to the Perplexed," in almost every respect the antithesis of the Zohar, influenced its own time
directly and openly; from the moment of its appearance
it affected people's minds, moving them to enthusiasm or
to consternation. Yet, after two centuries of a profound
influence, it began to lose its effectiveness more and more,
until finally, for centuries long, it vanished almost entirely

from the consciousness of the broad masses. It was only at the end of the 18th century that the Jewish Enlightenment again brought it into prominence, seeking to make it an active force in its own struggle.

It was different with the Zohar, which had to make its way out of an almost complete, hardly penetrable anonymity and concealment. For a hundred years and more it elicited scarcely any interest to speak of. When it came on the scene, it expressed (and therefore appealed to) the feeling of a very small class of men who in loosely organized conventicles strove for a new, mystical understanding of the world of Judaism, and who had not the faintest notion that this particular book alone, among the many which sought to express their new world-view in allegory and symbol, was destined to succeed. Soon, however, the light shadow of scandal that had fallen upon its publication and initial appearance in the world of literature, the enigma of the illegitimate birth of a literary forgery, disappeared and was forgotten. Very slowly but surely the influence of the Zohar grew; and when the groups among which it had gained dominion proved themselves in the storms of Jewish history to be the bearers of a new religious attitude that not only laid claim to, but in fact achieved, authority, then the Zohar in a late but exceedingly intensive afterglow of national life came to fulfil the great historical task of a sacred text supplementing the Bible and Talmud on a new level of religious consciousness. This inspirational character has been attached to it by numerous Jewish groups in Eastern Europe and the Orient down to our own days, nor have they hesitated to assert that final conclusion which has since earliest times been drawn in the recognition of a sacred text, namely, that the effect upon the soul of such a work is in the end not at all dependent upon its being understood.

It was only with the collapse of that stratum of life and belief in which the Kabbalah was able to represent a historical force that the splendor of the Zohar also faded; and later, in the revaluation of the Enlightenment, it became the "book of lies," considered to have obscured the pure light of Judaism. The reform-tending polemic in this case too made haste to become an instrument of historical criticism, which, it must be said, after a few promising starts, showed itself weak and uncertain in the carrying out of its program, sound as its methods and true as many of its theses may have been.

Historical criticism, however, will survive the brief immortality of that "genuine" Judaism whose view of history and whose hierarchy of values gave rise to it. Freed from polemic, and concerned for a more precise and objective insight into its subject matter, it will now assert itself in the new (and in part very old) context in which we begin to see the world of Judaism, and Judaism's history.

Literary Character

The Zohar in its external literary physiognomy seems far from being conceived and constructed as a unified composition. Still less can it be regarded as any kind of systematic exposition of the world-view of the Kabbalah, like many such which have come down to us from the period of the Kabbalah's origin and even more from later times. It is rather, in the printed form that lies before us, a collection of treatises and writings that are considerably different from one another in external form. Most of the sections seem to be interpretations of Bible passages, or short sayings or longer homilies, or else often artfully composed reports of whole series of homilies in which Rabbi Simeon ben Yohai, a famous teacher of the 2nd century, and his friends and students interpret the words of Scripture in accordance with their hidden meaning, and, moreover, almost always in the Aramaic language. Other sections, though these are few, have been preserved in the form of anonymous and purely factual accounts in which there can be recognized no such settings of landscape and persons as those described with so much care elsewhere in the work, often in highly dramatic fashion. Fairly often the exposition is enigmatically brief, but frequently the ideas are very fully presented with homiletical amplitude and an architectonically effective elaboration. Many sections actually appear as fragments of oracles and as reports of secret revelations, and are written in a peculiarly enthusiastic, a solemn, "elevated" style; so much so that the detached reader is apt to feel they have overstepped the bounds of good taste in the direction of affectation and bombast. While often the exposition has an only slightly elevated tone and is pregnant and realistic, we do find in a certain number of passages a passion for the association

of ideas which is pushed to an extreme, degenerating into
a flight from conceptual reality. Externally, also, many
parts are set off from the rest by special titles as more or
less independent compositions, and this not without very
good reason.

The main part of the Zohar, which is arranged by Pentateuch portions, purports to be an ancient Midrash, and in
many details it imitates the form of the ancient midrashic
works of the first centuries C.E. On the whole, indeed, it
breaks through this form and assumes the quite different
one of the medieval sermon. Such extended compositions,
constructed on a definite plan, as we find in the Zohar to
the length of fifteen or twenty or even forty pages, are
quite foreign to the ancient Midrash. Here a different principle of composition obtains. The same is true of the parts
called *Midrash ha-Neelam* (The Secret Midrash) and
Sitre Torah (Secrets of the Torah), which in a large number of Pentateuch portions, especially in the first book,
provide parallel pieces to the "main parts."

The Secret Midrash, to be sure, has much to say about
Simeon ben Yohai and his circle, but almost completely
avoids genuinely mystical and theosophical trains of
thought; instead, in its most important sections, it pre-
sents radical allegorizations of the patriarchal stories as
indicative of the fate of the soul before and after death.
These allegories very clearly reveal their kinship to the
philosophical homiletic of the 13th century. The Secrets
of the Torah, on the other hand, which in the main was
composed without the use of the Midrash form or the

addition of names, represents the transition from philosophical-eschatological allegory to genuinely mystical exegesis.

The *Idra Rabba* (The Great Assembly) describes, on an excellently constructed plan, the mystical "figure" of the Deity in the symbol of Primal Man, and Simeon ben Yohai treats the same theme a second time in a monologue before his death, an event which is most vividly described in *Idra Zutta* (The Small Assembly). Anonymous "Mishnayot" and "Toseftot," intended as introductions to other longer sections, expound oracles concerning the world and the soul. In *Raya Mehemna* (The Faithful Shepherd), Moses and Rabbi Simeon converse about the hidden reasons for the commandments. The *Tikkunim* again give a detailed interpretation of the first section of the Pentateuch, and thus we have more than a total of ten great and small parts that are evidently separate units. It is no wonder, therefore, that the question of the unity of the Zohar has found very uncertain answers.

Origin and Authorship

While the different points of view in Zohar criticism cannot be fully gone into here, the present status of research can, at any rate, be briefly summarized. The most radical opinion was put forth by Heinrich Graetz. He declared all parts of the Zohar without exception to be the work of the Spanish kabbalist Moses de Leon, who died in 1305, and the great historian emptied the vials of an exceedingly vehement wrath over him. Very few reputations have come down to posterity from the school of Graetz in so battered and pitiable a state as has de Leon's. Far from recognizing the genius that must have been at work in the Zohar, if it was the production of a single man, Graetz saw in it only deception and charlatanism.

In contrast to this view, the Zohar has been regarded, especially in the preceding generation, as a work altogether without unity, or else as one that grew anonymously in the course of time, and in which the most varied and often contradictory forces of the kabbalistic movement found expression. In either case, Moses de Leon was in this view regarded as the redactor of ancient writings and fragments, to which he may perhaps have added something of his own. The theory that "primitive" sources and documents have been preserved in the Zohar, although admittedly in revised form, is today widespread. Thus the Zohar (and this is undoubtedly what has gone to make this view so attractive though it lacks all proof) would really be, even in its external beginnings, a deposit of the creative folk-spirit and, like the Bible and Talmud, the anonymous work of centuries. And it may be taken as an indication of the enduring influence of the school of Ahad Haam that the lack of proof for this theory—and in its behalf not even the shadow of philological-critical evidence has been brought forward—has in no way seriously hindered its spread. What is plausible can do without proof.

Every attempt to establish, through the working out of exact criteria, that certain layers and parts of the Zohar go back to a time before the middle of the 13th century turns out to be new evidence to the contrary. This fact has been vividly experienced by the present writer. After devoting many years to just such an analysis, he found the unequivocal result to correspond so little to the expectations with which he started out, refuting them in fact so thoroughly, that he ventures to state with assurance the following conclusions.

The Zohar is, in the main, a unified book, although not so unified as Graetz imagined. Among the separate parts there are no strata or ancient material from mystical Midrashim unknown to us; on the contrary, these parts came out of the heads of their authors just as they are, except that many parts are undoubtedly missing, having disappeared from the manuscripts as early as the 14th century. Much of the printed text is wrongly arranged, where the manuscript, however, retains the correct order. Finally, a few shorter pieces were added still later in the 14th century. The separate parts do not relate to a corresponding number of strata or authors, but the whole corpus of Zohar literature was in origin made up of three strata. These, in themselves predominantly unified, are:

1) *Midrash ha-Neelam.*
2) The main part of the Zohar with the *Idra Rabba, Idra Zutta, Sitre Torah* and most of the other short treatises.
3) *Raya Mehemna* and the so-called *Tikkune Zohar,* both of which had a single author.

Certain it is that the author of the third stratum, who had the second before him in completed form and cites it

and rather unsuccessfully imitates it, is not the author of
the first two. Everything speaks against this being so: the
linguistic character of the third, its strongly apocalyptic
tendencies, its laborious construction, its divergent views,
and its way of using sources. One might perhaps propose
the rather hazardous thesis that we are here dealing with
the work of the old age and decline of the chief author,
whose early talents had left him and who was imitating
himself, were it not for the fact that too much of an independent nature inheres in the book *Tikkunim* to make this
thesis tenable. This last group of writings was composed
around 1300.

The first two strata, on the other hand, are in all prob-
ability by a single author, whose development from the
composition of the first to the second is still clearly trace-
able, and thus it becomes gratuitous to assume any break
in the identity of the person who stands behind the whole
production. The Secret Midrash, which has hitherto been
customarily regarded as the latest part of the whole work
because of its free use of philosophical terminology as well
as its partial use of the Hebrew language, is in all prob-
ability the earliest part.

Behind the whole stands the living personality of a
mystic who, starting with the philosophical and talmudic
education of his time, lets himself be ever more deeply
drawn to the mystical and gnostic ideas of the Kabbalah,
and finally gives up his philosophical interests altogether,
developing instead a truly astonishing genius for mystical
homiletics; indeed, half a millennium had to elapse before
Jewish literature was again able to show anything com-

parable. For such is the author of these most important
parts of the Zohar—no redactor or collector but a homiletic genius. It was Kabbalah, as it had developed before
his time, and having become his spiritual home, which he,
with unexpected and impressive power, constructed from
out of the text of Scripture and the ancient haggadic mo-
tifs of the Midrash.

Thus although his world of thought and concept was
not novel, his mystical sources were by no means forgotten
tomes and apocrypha from obscure centuries. They were
the literature of the Kabbalah to the time of Moses ben
Nahman (1195–1270) and his circle, a literature which
has been in large part preserved and is today quite well
known. The manner in which this Zohar author's mystical
world was constructed reveals to us very precisely the only
period of time in which he is to be correctly placed in the
development of the Kabbalah; in addition to which a
whole series of linguistic and factual criteria, quite independent of one another, point to exactly the same time. It
was certainly around 1280 that these main parts of the
Zohar were composed in Spain by a kabbalist who had not
seen Palestine. In ever new guises and externally different
literary and stylistic forms this work erupts from an author
who seems to have deeply experienced his conversion to
kabbalism. But in spite of all the masks which he is fond
of putting on, the inner form and the personal style are
always identical.

But what about these masks? What about this whole
Galilean landscape, which dissolves into unreality, and
Rabbi Simeon ben Yohai, his family and friends, and all

the other trappings of a Midrash-like finery, in which the
author seems to find so much pleasure, as if enjoying himself in the play of fantasy? This flight into pseudonymity
and romantic backdrop evoked in the critical writings of
the 19th century a literary excitement—angry attacks and
moralistic condemnation, as well as a circumspect and
sometimes vociferous apologetic—which seems to us today
to have been considerably exaggerated. For a long time we
have known that literary forgeries represent a flight into
anonymity and pseudonymity just as often as they indicate
trickery; and not for nothing have we retained the foreign
work "pseudepigrapha" to designate in particular a legiti-
mate category of religious literature, by a term devoid of
the moralistic undertone of reprobation which echoes in
the English word "forgery." Important documents of our
religious literature are in this sense forgeries; also, the
mystical literature which the author of the Zohar may have
read consisted, to a considerable extent, of earlier pseudepigrapha.

We are not even sure whether the author, who handles
the technique of pseudepigraphy with so much virtuosity
and permits the persons of his dialogue a profusion of in-
vented book titles and citations, took the literary form of
the kabbalistic pseudepigrapha very seriously. Certainly,
in a whole series of imitations of the Zohar which appeared during the first hundred years after its publication,
it is clear that their authors did not by any means take the
masquerade for the real thing. The masquerade served as a
welcome means of letting the chance name of an author
who found himself in possession of secret wisdom disap-

pear behind his material, and if the framework is sometimes overdecorated by wilful or, it may be, reckless hands
—and the Zohar is the most important but by far not the
only example of such love of masquerade in Jewish literature—still this was only an added touch. Only later were
these things more crudely conceived, when the disguise became a historical reality.

How playfully the author of the Zohar himself used this
form is shown by the noteworthy fact that together with
this book he composed still other shorter pseudepigraphic
works, of which one, the so-called "Testament of Rabbi
Eliezer the Great," has enjoyed the good fortune of being
among the most widely circulated Jewish folk-books, although its true origin has gone generally unrecognized.
Graetz, indeed, has pictured Moses de Leon to us as forg-
ing the Zohar out of greed for profit, in order to make
money out of the gullible rich after the books published
under his own name had ceased to yield him sufficient
gain. This storybook figure of a cunning rogue would be
unacceptable to historical criticism even if we did not have
conclusive proof that the main part of the Zohar was in
existence before 1286, the year that Moses de Leon wrote
his "own" first book, which was entirely based upon the
Zohar. This does not, of course, exclude the possibility of
his having written the Zohar himself previous to that year.

But was Moses de Leon in fact the author of this very
Zohar, as even his own contemporaries long ago sus-
pected? We may now say with a fair amount of philo-
logical certainty that Moses de Leon must indeed be considered the actual author of the book. True, while much

former evidence bolstering that hypothesis has been disproved, there has now come to light certain entirely new evidence to speak decisively for Moses de Leon's authorship. This much is certain: Moses de Leon was in possession of the original work and circulated it from 1280 on, so that a countryman of his, Isaac ibn Sahula of Guadalajara read The Secret Midrash as early as 1281. From 1286 on Moses de Leon composed his "own" writings in very considerable number. These books reveal an author who lives and moves wholly in the specific world of the Zohar and not merely in the general world of the contemporary Kabbalah, so that we have only the choice of saying either that he entirely surrendered himself to the stronger personality of the nameless author of the Zohar, to the extent of giving up his own personal traits, or that he himself was the author. For the latter view there is a noteworthy chronological indication. Up until recently, no one knew how old Moses de Leon was when he began to write, or whether it was at all possible to fit into his "pre-history," before he began to write under his own name, those ten to twenty years which must have been at the very least required for the conception of a work of the kind to which the first two strata of the Zohar belong. But before the First World War, there was found in Moscow a manuscript which by a strange coincidence was none other than one of the scripts of Maimonides' "Guide to the Perplexed," and had been written for Moses de Leon in 1264. These twenty "empty" years (1264 to 1286) preceding his public appearance fit in very strikingly indeed with the period of the origin of the Zohar, which has been determined through quite different connections and criteria. Would not the path that led from the reading of the "Guide to the Perplexed" to the eschatological mysticism of Moses de Leon's "Book of the Rational Soul" be the very one which was described above as that of the inner development of the Zohar's author, from half-philosophical allegory to the mystical-theosophical interpretation of Scripture? We may say with certitude that no one of the other Spanish kabbalists of that period who are within our ken and appear before us with their individual spiritual traits can be brought into the question as a possible author of the Zohar. Neither Abraham Abulafia nor Moses of Burgos, neither Jacob of Segovia nor Joseph Gikatila shows that unmistakable physiognomy. And whoever is unwilling to believe in the Great Unknown who has so successfully eluded all attempts to trace him, must give his adherence to Moses de Leon, if he wishes to succeed in the reconstruction of one of the most significant and clearly marked figures of Jewish religious history.

Something must here be said about the language of the Zohar, which has proved to be one of the most important factors in its influence. The sustained chiaroscuro of this peculiar Zohar-Aramaic has overlaid with a venerable patina and a luster of restrained enthusiasm ideas which, if they had been expressed in the sober Hebrew of the 13th century, would have had to speak by themselves; in the form which they assumed, they have, one might say, found their native idiom. This linguistic achievement is the more admirable in that the medieval Hebrew, as is evident to a keen eye, shows through the Aramaic on page after page, in word order, syntax and terminology; and the more admirable also, considering that the Aramaic vocabulary of the author evidences a curious poverty and simplicity. As soon as one has read thirty pages of the original, one knows the language of the whole book well enough, and in this same respect it is astonishing with what modest resources so much has been expressed and so great an effect has been achieved. Often enough the exact understanding of a passage in the Zohar is dependent upon a retranslation into the Hebrew of the contemporary Kabbalah, and Moses de Leon's writings above all quickly give the key to many passages. A good many mystical concepts are expressed rather arbitrarily in new word-formations, which in many cases have arisen from corrupted forms of talmudic words in medieval manuscripts, or from similar misunderstandings.

On the Selection for This Volume

It would seem to be nothing less than presumptuous to offer any selection from such a work as the Zohar, and, certainly, it is difficult to focus into a brief book anything like the richness of content, the plenitude of ideas inhering in the original. Indeed, no selection can assume the task of portraying the mystical doctrine of the Zohar. Such a presentation—if at all feasible within the compass of a small volume—would require an apparatus of explanatory notes and comments of no less size than the body of text.

What I have therefore attempted to present in the pages following is a sequence of passages which might be expected to arouse an immediate interest in the reader: by the colorfulness with which the life of the soul is pictured, by the curious poignancy of scriptural exegesis, by the outright paradoxicality of the thoughts asserted.

All the passages selected—some given in a slightly condensed form—have in common their direct appeal to the imagination and fantasy of the reader, an appeal not dependent on the interpretation of the numerous technical and symbolical associations in which the texts abound. Some absolutely necessary explanations are provided in the footnotes. On the whole, however, I ventured to assume that the interested reader would himself desire to reflect on the profuse symbols and images as they appear herein. It was in such manner that the Zohar did appeal to wider circles of readers through the ages. It matters little whether this or that symbolic connotation is properly recognized, or not.

With the foregoing in mind, I selected such passages as would throw light on the mystical ideas concerning God, together with the various stages of his manifestation, and on the idea of the soul, its grades and its destiny, as taught by the Zohar. In a number of instances, one passage may find elucidation by another.

Nor did I deem it wise to arrange the volume according to themes and topics. Such an organization does not recommend itself, inasmuch as all the passages selected are broadly interrelated, one being connected and bound up with another. Thus it was found advisable to follow, on the whole, the same sequence in which the pieces appear in the original text of the Zohar.

This small volume will have fulfilled its task if it succeeds in conveying to the reader some notion of the power of contemplative fantasy and creative imagery hidden within the seemingly abstruse thinking of the kabbalists.

G. G. S.

GENESIS

THE BEGINNING

"In the beginning" [Gen. 1: 1]—when the will of the King began to take effect, he engraved signs into the heavenly sphere [that surrounded him]. Within the most hidden recess a dark flame issued from the mystery of *eyn sof*, the Infinite, like a fog forming in the unformed —enclosed in the ring of that sphere, neither white nor black, neither red nor green, of no color whatever. Only after this flame began to assume size and dimension, did it produce radiant colors. From the innermost center of the flame sprang forth a well out of which colors issued and spread upon everything beneath, hidden in the mysterious hiddenness of *eyn sof*.

The well broke through and yet did not break through the ether [of the sphere]. It could not be recognized at all until a hidden, supernal point shone forth under the impact of the final breaking through.*

Beyond this point nothing can be known. Therefore it is called *reshit*, beginning—the first word [out of the ten] by means of which the universe has been created.

* This primordial point is identified by the Zohar with the wisdom of God [*hokhmah*], the ideal thought of Creation.

When King Solomon "penetrated into the depths of the nut garden," as it is written, "I descended into the garden of nuts" [Cant. 6:11], he took up a nut shell and studying it, he saw an analogy in its layers with the spirits which motivate the sensual desires of humans, as it is written, "and the delights of the sons of men [are from] male and female demons" [Eccles. 2:8].

The Holy One, be blessed, saw that it was necessary to put into the world all of these things so as to make sure of permanence, and of having, so to speak, a brain surrounded by numerous membranes. The whole world, upper and lower, is organized on this principle, from the primary mystic center to the very outermost of all the layers. All are coverings, the one to the other, brain within brain, spirit inside of spirit, shell within shell.

The primal center is the innermost light, of a translucence, subtility, and purity beyond comprehension. That inner point extended becomes a "palace" which acts as an enclosure for the center, and is also of a radiance translucent beyond the power to know it.

The "palace" vestment for the incognizable inner point, while it is an unknowable radiance in itself, is nevertheless of a lesser subtility and translucency than the primal point. The "palace" extends into a vestment for itself, the primal light. From then outward, there is extension upon extension, each constituting a vesture to the one before, as a membrane to the brain. Though membrane first, each extension becomes brain to the next extension.

Likewise does the process go on below; and after this design, man in the world combines brain and membrane, spirit and body, all to the more perfect ordering of the world. When the moon was conjoined with the sun, she was luminous, but when she went apart from the sun and was given governance of her own hosts, her status and her light were reduced, and shell after shell was fashioned for investing the brain, and all was for its good.

THE FIRST LIGHT

"And God said, Let there be light, and there was light" [Gen. 1:3].

This is the primal light which God made. It is the light of the eye. This light God showed to Adam, and by means of it he was enabled to see from end to end of the world. This light God showed to David, and he, beholding it, sang forth his praise, saying, "Oh how abundant is Thy goodness, which Thou hast laid up for them that fear Thee" [Ps. 31:20]. This is the light through which God revealed to Moses the land of Israel from Gilead to Dan.

Foreseeing the rise of three sinful generations, the generation of Enoch, the generation of the Flood, and the generation of the Tower of Babel, God put away the light from their enjoyment. Then he gave it to Moses in the time that his mother was hiding him, for the first three months after his birth. When Moses was taken before

Pharaoh, God took it from him, and did not give it again until he stood upon the mount of Sinai to receive the Torah. Thenceforth Moses had it for his until the end of his life, and therefore he could not be approached by the Israelites until he had put a veil upon his face [Exod. 34:33].

"Let there be light, and there was light" [Gen. 1:3]. To whatsoever the word *vayehi* [and there was] is applied, that thing is in this world and in the world to come.

Rabbi Isaac said: At the Creation, God irradiated the world from end to end with the light, but then it was withdrawn, so as to deprive the sinners of the world of its enjoyment, and it is stored away for the righteous, as it stands written, "Light is sown for the righteous" [Ps. 97:11]; then will the worlds be in harmony and all will be united into one, but until the future world is set up, this light is put away and hidden. This light emerged from the darkness which was hewed out by the strokes of the Most Secret; and likewise, from the light which was hidden away, through some secret path, there was hewed out the darkness of the lower world in which inheres light. This lower darkness is called "night" in the verse, "and the darkness He called night" [Gen. 1:5].

Rabbi Simeon then rose and spoke: In meditating, I have perceived that when God was about to create man, then above and below all creatures commenced to tremble. The course of the sixth day was unfolding when at last the divine decision was made. Then there blazed forth the source of all lights and opened up the gate of the East, from where light flows. The light which had been bestowed on it at the beginning, the South gave forth in full glory, and the South took hold upon the East. The East took hold on the North, and the North awakened and, opening forth, called loud to the West that he should come to him. Then the West traveled up into the North and came together with it, and after that the South took hold on the West, and the North and the South surrounded the Garden, being its fences. Then the East drew near to the West, and the West was gladdened and it said, "Let us make man in our image, after our likeness" [Gen. 1:26], to embrace like us the four quarters and the higher and the lower. Thereupon were East and West united, and produced man. Therefore have our sages said that man arose out from the site of the Temple.

Moreover, we may regard the words "Let us make man" as conveying this: to the lower beings who derived from the side of the upper world God disclosed the secret of how to form the divine name Adam, in which is encompassed the upper and the lower, in the force of its three letters *alef*, *dalet*, and *mem* final. When the three letters had come down below, there was perceived in their form, complete, the name Adam, to comprehend male and female. The female was fastened to the side of the male, and God cast the male into a deep slumber, and he lay on the site of the Temple. God then cut the female from him and decked her as a bride and led her to him, as it is written, "And he took one of his sides, and closed up the place with flesh" [Gen. 2:21]. In the ancient books, I have seen it said that here the word "one" means "one woman," that is, the original Lilith, who lay with him and from him conceived. But up to that time, she was no help to him, as it is said, "but for Adam there was not found an help meet for him" [Gen. 2:20]. Adam, then, was the very last, for it was right that he should find the world complete when he made his appearance.

"No shrub of the field was yet in the earth" [Gen. 2:5].

Rabbi Simeon went on to say: The allusion is to the magnificent trees which grew later, but as yet were minute. Adam and Eve, as we have said, were created side by side. Why not face to face? For the reason that heaven and earth were not yet in complete harmony, "the Lord God had not caused it to rain upon the earth" [Gen. 2:5]. When the lower union was rendered perfect, and Adam and Eve turned face to face, then was the upper union perfected.

This we may know from the matter of the Tabernacle: for we have learned that together with it there was put up another tabernacle, nor was the upper one raised until the lower one was erected; and so it was in this case. Moreover, inasmuch as all above was not yet perfectly ordered, Adam and Eve were not created face to face. This is borne out by the order of the verses in the Scripture; first it is written, "For the Lord God had not caused it to rain upon the earth," and following, "there was not a man to till the ground" [*ibid.*], and it signifies that man was yet imperfect, for only when Eve was made perfect, was he then made perfect too. Further proof is that in the word *vayisgor* [and he closed], there occurs for the first time in this passage the letter *samekh,* which signifies "support," as much as to say that male and female they now supported the one the other. In like wise, do the lower world and the upper sustain each other. Not until the lower world was made perfect, was the other world also made perfect. When the lower world was made to support the upper, by being turned face to face with it, the world was then finished, for previously "the Lord God had not caused it to rain upon the earth."

Then, "There went up a mist from the earth" [Gen. 2:6], to make up for the lack, by "watering the whole face of the ground" [*ibid.*]; and the mist rising is the yearning of the female for the male. Yet another interpretation says that we take the word "not" from the first verse to use in the second with "mist," and this means that God failed to send rain because a mist had not gone up, for from below must come the impulse to move the power above. Thus, to form the cloud, vapor ascends first from the earth. And likewise, the smoke of the sacrifice ascends, creating harmony above, and the uniting of all, and so the celestial sphere has completion in it. It is from below that the movement starts, and thereafter is all perfected. If the Community of Israel failed to initiate the impulse, the One above would also not move to go to her, and it is thus the yearning from below which brings about the completion above.

Rabbi Simeon set out one time for Tiberias, and with him were Rabbi Yose, Rabbi Judah, and Rabbi Hiyya. On the road coming toward them they met Rabbi Phineas. All dismounted and sat down on the mountainside, under a tree. Rabbi Phineas spoke: While we sit, I should like to hear some of those wondrous ideas which figure in your discourse daily.

Then Rabbi Simeon spoke, commencing with the text, "And he went on his journeys from the South even to Beth-el, unto the place where his tent had been at the beginning, between Beth-el and Ai" [Gen. 13:3]. He said: We might here have expected the word journey; but instead we read "journeys," which is intended to mean that on the journey with him was the Divine Presence. It behooves a man to be "male and female," always, so that his faith may remain stable, and in order that the Presence may never leave him. You will ask: How with the man who makes a journey, and, away from his wife, ceases to be "male and female"? Such a one, before starting, and while he still is "male and female," must pray to God, to draw unto himself the Presence of his Master. After he has prayed and offered thanksgiving, and when the Presence is resting on him, then he may go, for by virtue of his union with the Presence he is now male and female in the country, just as he was male and female in the town, for it is written: "Righteousness [zedek, feminine of zaddik] shall go before him and shall make his footsteps a way" [Ps. 85:14].

Remark this. The whole time of his traveling a man should heed well his actions, lest the holy union break off, and he be left imperfect, deprived of the union with the female. If it was needful when he and his wife were together, how much greater the need when the heavenly mate is with him? And the more so, indeed, since this heavenly union acts as his constant guard on his journey, until his return home. Moreover, it is his duty, once back home, to give his wife pleasure, inasmuch as she it was who obtained for him the heavenly union.

There is twofold reason for this duty of cohabitation. First, this pleasure is a religious one, giving joy also to the Divine Presence, and it is an instrument for peace in the world, as it stands written, "and thou shalt know that thy tent is in peace; and thou shalt visit thy habitation and not sin" [Job 5:24]. (It may be questioned, is it a sin if he fails to go in to his wife? It is a sin, for in his failure, he detracts from the honor of the heavenly mate who was given him by reason of his wife.) Secondly, if his wife should conceive, the heavenly partner bestows upon the child a holy soul; for this covenant is called the covenant of the Holy One, be blessed.

Hence, a man should be as zealous to enjoy this joy as to enjoy the joy of the Sabbath, at which time is consummated the union of the sages with their wives. Thus, "thou shalt know that thy tent is in peace," for the Presence accompanies you and sojourns in your house, and for this reason "thou shalt visit thy habitation and not sin," in gladly carrying out the religious duty to have conjugal intercourse before the Presence.

So it is that the students of Torah, away from their wives the six days of the week they engage in study, are in this period attached to a heavenly mate, so that they do not cease to be "male and female." And with the incoming of the Sabbath, it behooves them to rejoice their wives, to the honor of the heavenly union, and in seeking to do the will of their Master, as has been stated.

In like wise, when a man's wife is in her days of separation, in those days while he waits for her the man has with him the heavenly mate, so that he continues to be "male and female." When the wife is purified, the man is in duty bound to rejoice her, in the joyful fulfillment of a religious obligation. The same reasons we have given apply also in this case.

According to secret doctrine, the mystics are bound to give their whole mind and purpose to the one [the Shekhinah]. It may be objected that in the light of the previous argument, a man is in a state of more honor on a journey than at home, by virtue of the heavenly mate who is then with him. This is not so. At home, the wife is the foundation of a man's house, inasmuch as it is by virtue of her that the Presence does not leave the house.

So the verse, "and Isaac brought her into his mother Sarah's tent" [Gen. 24:67], our masters have interpreted to mean that the Divine Presence came to Isaac's house along with Rebecca. According to secret doctrine, the supernal Mother is together with the male only when the house is in readiness and at that time the male and female are conjoined. At such time blessings are showered forth by the supernal Mother upon them.

Likewise, the lower Mother is found together with the male only when the house is in readiness, and the male goes in to the female and they conjoin together; then the blessings of the lower Mother are showered forth for them. Therefore, two females, his Mother and his wife, are to compass a man about in his house, like the Male above. There is reference to this in the verse "Unto [*ad*] the desire of the everlasting hills" [Gen. 49:26]. This *ad* is the desired object of the "everlasting hills," by which is meant the supreme female, who is to make ready for him, and make him blissful and bless him, and also the lower female, who is to be joined in union with him and take support from him.

Likewise below, the desire of the "everlasting hills" is for the man when he is married, and two females, one of the upper, one of the lower world, are to give him bliss—the upper one in showering upon him all blessings and the lower one in receiving support from him and being joined together with him. So it is with the man in his house. But when he is on a journey, while the supernal Mother is still with him, the lower wife remains behind; and therefore on his returning, it behooves him to do that which will compass him about with two females, as we have explained.

Rabbi Simeon said: In one place it is written, "For the Lord thy God is a consuming fire" [Deut. 4:24], and elsewhere, "But ye that cleave unto the Lord your God are alive every one of you this day" [Deut. 4:4]. The Companions have already discussed the seeming inconsistency between these texts, but I offer yet another interpretation.

It has been affirmed by the Companions that there exists a sort of fire which is stronger than other fire, and the one consumes and annihilates the other. If we continue this thought, it can be said that he who cares to pierce into the mystery of the holy unity of God should consider the flame as it rises from a burning coal or candle.

There must always be some material substance from which the flame thus rises. In the flame itself may be seen two lights: the one white and glowing, the other black, or blue. Of the two, the white light is the higher and rises unwavering. Underneath it is the blue or black light upon which the other rests as on a support. The two are conjoined, the white reposing upon the throne of the black. The blue or black base is, likewise, connected to something beneath it, which feeds it and makes it to cling to the white light above. At times this blue or black light turns red, but the light above remains constantly white. This lower light, at times black, at times blue, at times red, serves to link the white light above it with the material substance below to which it is bound and through which it keeps kindled. This lower light is in its nature an instrument for destruction and death, devouring whatever comes near it.

But the white light above neither consumes nor demolishes, nor does it ever change.

Therefore Moses said, "For the Lord thy God is a consuming fire" [Deut. 4:24], consuming, actually, all that is beneath him; for this reason he said "thy God" and not "our God," inasmuch as Moses stood in the supernal light which does not consume and does not demolish.

Remark further. It is Israel alone which impels the blue light to kindle and to link itself with the white light, Israel, who cleave to the blue light from below. And though it be in the nature of the blue or black light to destroy whatever it touches beneath, yet Israel, cleaving to it from beneath, are not destroyed; so it is said, "But ye that cleave unto the Lord your God are alive every one of you this day." *Your* God and not *our* God; that is to say, it is the blue or black flame, consuming and annihilating whatever cleaves to it from below, and still you cleave and are alive.

Only just perceptible above the white light and encompassing it, is yet another light, this one symbolizing the supreme essence. So does the aspiring flame symbolize the supernal mysteries of wisdom.

Rabbi Phineas went to him and kissed him, and said, Blessed be God who guided me here. And they went out with Rabbi Phineas, accompanying him for three miles. When they had returned, Rabbi Simeon spoke: The description I have given may be taken as a symbol of the holy unity of God. In the holy name YHVH,* the second

* The four letters of the name of God represent four stages of ever increasing divine manifestation.

letter *hé* is the blue or black light attached to the remaining letters *yod, hé, vav,* which constitute the luminous white light. But there come times when this blue light is not *hé* but *dalet,* which is to say, poverty; this means, when Israel fail to cleave to it from beneath and it in turn fails therefore to burn and cleave to the white light, the blue light is *dalet,* but when Israel make it to cleave to the white light, then it is *hé*. If male and female are not together, than *hé* is erased and there remains only *dalet* [poverty]. But when the chain is perfect, the *hé* cleaves to the white light, and Israel cleave to the *hé* and give substance for its light, and are yet not destroyed.

In this we see the mystery of the sacrifice. The rising smoke kindles the blue light, which then joins itself to the white light, whereupon the entire candle is wholly kindled, alight with a single unified flame. As it is the nature of the blue light to demolish whatever comes into touch with it from beneath, therefore if the sacrifice be acceptable and the candle wholly kindled, then, as with Elijah, "the fire of the Lord descends and consumes the burnt-offering" [I Kings 18: 38], and this reveals that the chain is perfected, for then the blue light cleaves to the white light above, while at the same time consuming the fat and flesh of the burnt-offering beneath, nor can it consume what is below, except it rise and join itself to the white light. At such time, peace reigns in all worlds, and all together form a unity.

The blue light having devoured every thing beneath, the priests, the Levites, and the laity gather at its base with singing and meditation and with prayer, while above them the lamp glows, the lights are merged into a unity, worlds are illumined, and above and below, all are blessed. Therefore it is written, "ye, even while cleaving to the Lord your God, are alive every one of you this day." The word *atem* [you] is here preceded by the letter *vav* [and], which indicates that while the fat and flesh cleaving to the flame are devoured by it, you who cleave to it are yet alive.

As a man is in his hour to go from life, Adam, the first man, comes before him and asks him why he is departing from the world, and in what condition. The man says: Woe to thee that I must die on account of thee.

Adam answers: My son, one commandment did I break, and was punished for it; see how many are the commandments of your Master, both to do and not to do, that you have transgressed.

Said Rabbi Hiyya: To this day Adam exists, and two times each day he stands before the patriarchs and confesses his transgressions, and shows them the place where once he dwelled in heavenly glory.

Rabbi Yesa said: Adam comes before every man at the moment he is about to leave this life, in order to declare that the man is dying not because of Adam's sin, but on account of his own sins, as the sages said: "There is no death without sin."

THE THREE STRANDS OF SPIRIT

"And Noah begot three sons" [Gen. 6: 10].

Rabbi Hiyya said to Rabbi Judah: About this text, I will tell you what I have heard. This may be compared to a man who went into the recesses of a cave, and two or three children emerged together, widely diverse in character and comportment; one being virtuous, a second evil-doing, a third ordinary. Likewise, there are three strands of spirit, moving hither and thither, and they are drawn into three different worlds. *Neshamah* [super-soul]* issues forth and goes in among the mountain passages and there is joined by *ruah* [spirit]. Then it descends below, and here *nefesh* [vital soul]† joins *ruah,* and the three are linked into a unity.‡

Rabbi Judah said: *Nefesh* and *ruah* are conjoined, while *neshamah* has its abode in the character of a man, which place remains unknown and undiscovered. If a man strive to a pure life, he is therein assisted by holy *neshamah,* through the which he is made pure and saintly and attains to the name of holy. But if he does not strive to be righteous and pure of life, there does not animate him holy *neshamah,* but only the two grades, *nefesh* and *ruah.* More than that, he who enters into impurity is led further into it, and he is deprived of heavenly aid. Thus, each is moved forward upon the way which he takes.

* *Neshamah,* the "holy soul," super-soul, is the deepest intuitive power, which leads to the secrets of God and the universe.
† *Nefesh* is the soul proper, the natural soul given to every man.
‡ On the names and grades of the soul, see also the passages, Faith *and* The Three Aspects of the Soul.

The "soul" [*nefesh*] stands in intimate relation to the body, nourishing and upholding it; it is below, the first stirring. Having acquired due worth, it becomes the throne for the "spirit" [*ruah*] to rest upon, as it is written, "until the spirit be poured upon us from on high" [Isa. 32:15]. And when these two, soul and spirit, have duly readied themselves, they are worthy to receive the "super-soul" [*neshamah*], resting in turn upon the throne of the spirit [*ruah*]. The super-soul stands preëminent, and not to be perceived. There is throne upon throne, and for the highest a throne.

The study of these grades of the soul yields an understanding of the higher wisdom; and it is in such fashion that wisdom alone affords the linking together of a number of mysteries. It is *nefesh,* the lowest stirring, to which the body adheres; just as in a candle flame, the obscure light at the bottom adheres close to the wick, without which it cannot be. When fully kindled, it becomes a throne for the white light above it, and when these two come into their full glow, the white light becomes a throne for a light not wholly discernible, an unknowable essence reposing on the white light, and so in all there comes to be a perfect light.

It is the same with the man that arrives at perfection and is named "holy," as the verse says, "for the holy that are in the earth" [Ps. 16:3]. It is likewise in the upper world. Thus, when Abram entered the land, God appeared before him, and Abram received *nefesh* and there erected

an altar to the like grade [of divinity]. Then he "journeyed toward the South" [Gen. 12:9], and received *ruah*.
He attained at last to the summit of cleaving to God
through *neshamah*, and thereupon he "built an altar to
the Lord," whereby is meant the ineffable grade which is
that of *neshamah*. Then seeing that he must put himself
to the test, and pass through the grades, he journeyed into
Egypt. There he resisted being seduced by the demonic
essences, and when he had proved himself, he returned to
his abode; and, actually, he "went up out of Egypt" [Gen.
13:1], his faith was strong and reassured, and he attained
to the highest grade of faith. From that time, Abram
knew the higher wisdom, and cleaved to God, and of the
world he became the right hand.

MIDNIGHT

Rabbi Abba set out from Tiberias to go to the house of
his father-in-law. With him was his son, Rabbi Jacob.
When they arrived at Kfar Tarsha, they stopped to spend
the night. Rabbi Abba inquired of his host: Have you a
cock here? The host said: Why? Said Rabbi Abba: I wish
to rise at exactly midnight. The host replied: A cock is
not needed. By my bed is a water-clock. The water drips
out drop by drop, until just at midnight it is all out, and
then the wheel whirls back with a clatter which rouses the
entire household. This clock I made for a certain old man
who was in the habit of getting up each night at midnight

to study Torah. To this Rabbi Abba said: Blessed be God for guiding me here.

The wheel of the clock whirled back at midnight, and Rabbi Abba and Rabbi Jacob arose. They listened to the voice of their host coming up from the lower part of the house where he was sitting with his two sons, and saying: It is written, "Midnight I will rise to give thanks unto Thee for Thy righteous judgments" [Ps. 119:62]. The word "at" is not used, and so we assume that "Midnight" is an appellation of the Holy One, be blessed, whom David speaks to thus because midnight is the hour when He appears with his retinue, and goes into the Garden of Eden to converse with the righteous. Rabbi Abba then said to Rabbi Jacob: Now we indeed have the luck to be with the Presence.

And they went and seated themselves by their host, and said: Tell us again that which you just said, which is very good. Where did you hear it? He replied: My grandfather told it me. He said that the accuser angels below are busy all about the world during the first three hours of the night, but exactly at midnight the accusations halt, for at this moment God enters the Garden of Eden.

He continued: These ceremonies above occur nightly only at the exact midnight and this we know from what is written of Abraham, that "the night was divided for them" [Gen. 14:15] and from the verse "and it came to pass at the midnight," in the story of the Exodus [Exod. 12:29], and from numerous other passages in the Scripture. David knew it, so the old man related, because upon it depended his kingship. And so he was accustomed to

get up at this hour and sing praises, and on this account
he addressed God as "Midnight." He said, too, "I will
rise to give thanks unto Thee for Thy righteous judgments," since he knew this sphere to be the source of
justice, with judgments of earthly kings deriving therefrom, and for this reason David did not ever fail to rise
and sing praises at this hour.

Rabbi Abba went up to him and kissed him, and said:
Surely, it is as you say. Blessed be God who has guided me
here. In all places judgment is executed at night, and this
we have certainly affirmed, discussing it before Rabbi
Simeon.

At this, the young son of the innkeeper asked: Why
then does it say "Midnight"?

Rabbi Abba replied: It is established that the heavenly
King rises at midnight.

The boy said: I have a different explanation.

Then Rabbi Abba said: Speak, my child, because
through your mouth will speak the voice of the Lamp.*

He answered: This is what I have heard. Truly, night
is the time of strict judgment, a judgment which reaches
out impartially everywhere. But midnight draws from two
sides, from judgment and from mercy, the first half only
of the night being the period of judgment, while the second half takes illumination from the side of mercy
[*hesed*]. Wherefore David said "Midnight."

Upon this, Rabbi Abba stood up and put his hands on
the boy's head and blessed him, and said: I had thought

---

* Throughout the Zohar, Rabbi Simeon ben Yohai is called "the
holy lamp."

that wisdom dwells only in a few privileged pious men. But I perceive that even children are gifted with heavenly wisdom in the generation of Rabbi Simeon. Happy are you, Rabbi Simeon! Woe to the generation when you will have left it!

JACOB'S BLESSING

The blessings of Jacob, bestowed on him at various times, were indeed many. First, with the use of craftiness, he was enabled to have the blessings from his father; and returning from Laban, he received a blessing from the Divine Presence, as it is written, "And God [*Elohim*] blessed Jacob" [Gen. 35:9]; still another blessing was bestowed on him by the very guardian angel of Esau; and, again, when he set out for Padan-Aram, his father blessed him in this wise, "And God Almighty bless thee . . ." [Gen. 28:3].

Then Jacob, seeing he had all these blessings for his use, considered the matter, pondering, Now which among these blessings shall I first make use of? Then he decided at the time to avail himself of the last one, which was also the least of them. For, while he knew it to be weighty in itself, yet he regarded it as the least powerful in its prospect of dominion in this world. Therefore said Jacob: This blessing I shall make use of right now, the others I will keep in store for use in the time that I and after me my descendants shall have need for them, that is to say, the time when the nations will all come together in order to wipe out my posterity from the world.

Suitable to Jacob are the words: "All nations compass me about; verily, in the name of the Lord I will cut them off. They compass me about, yea, they compass me about. . . . They compass me about like bees" [Ps. 118:10–12]. Three times we see the words "compass me about," which correspond to the three other blessings: his father's first blessing, God's blessing, and third, the blessing of the angel.

Jacob said: When the time comes to go against the many kings and nations, then these benedictions will be needed; so shall I keep them in store for that time, but for dealing with Esau, this blessing will avail me.

He may be compared to a king having at his command great cohorts of soldiers led by able chieftains who stand prepared to engage in combat against the strongest foe. The king is told that a highway robber molests the countryside, and he gives orders: Let my gatekeepers be sent out against him. He is asked: Have you none others to send, of all your numerous cohorts, but these gatekeepers? He answers: They will do against the robber. A time will come when I shall need to engage with a mighty enemy, and against that time I must hold my troops and chieftains.

So said Jacob: Against Esau these blessings are sufficient, but the other blessings I must reserve until such time as my descendants will need them to take their stand against the great ones and rulers of the earth.

When that time comes, these blessings will begin to

work, and the world will be in harmony. From then on, the one kingdom will supervene over all the other kingdoms, and it will endure for ever, as it is written: "It shall break in pieces and consume all these kingdoms, but it shall stand for ever" [Dan. 2:44]. . . .

In connection with Jacob's blessings, Rabbi Hiyya quoted the verse, "A remnant shall return, even the remnant of Jacob" [Isa. 10:21]. Rabbi Hiyya said: This refers to the remaining blessings. It is further written, "And the remnant of Jacob shall be in the midst of many peoples, as dew from the Lord, as showers upon the grass" [Micah 5:6].

Rabbi Yesa said: It is written, "A son honoureth his father and a servant his master" [Mal. 1:6]. Esau was a son such as this, for no man in the world did so greatly honor his father as Esau, which indeed gained for him dominion in this world. Eliezer the servant of Abraham exemplified the honor given by "a servant his master." Moreover, Israel became subject to Esau on account of the tears which Esau shed, and this to be so until, weeping, they return to the Holy One, be blessed, as it says, "They shall come with weeping" [Jer. 31:9]. At that time there will be fulfilled the prophecy: "And saviours shall come up on mount Zion, to judge the mount of Esau; and the kingdom shall be the Lord's" [Obad. 1:21]. Blessed be the Lord for evermore.

Sitting one day at the gate of Lydda, Rabbi Abba saw a man approach and seat himself on a ledge which jutted out over the hollow ground far beneath. The man was weary with travel, and fell asleep. Rabbi Abba beheld a serpent crawling toward the man, and it had almost reached him when a branch hurtled from a tree and killed it. Now the man awakened, and, seeing the serpent before him, he jumped up; at this instant the ledge collapsed and crashed into the hollow below.

Rabbi Abba approached the man and said: Tell me, why has God seen fit to perform two miracles for you, what have you done?

To which the man answered: Whosoever wronged me, at any time, always I made peace with him and forgave him. And if I failed to effect peace with him, then I refrained from going to take my rest before I forgave him, and along with him, forgave any others who had vexed me; at no time did I brood on the injury the man had done to me; rather, I made special efforts of kindness from then on to such a man.

At this Rabbi Abba wept and said: This man surpasses even Joseph in his deeds; that Joseph should have been forbearing toward his brethren and shown them compassion was only natural, but this man has done more, and it is meet that the Holy One, be blessed, work successive miracles for him.

After this Rabbi Abba discoursed on the verse: "He that walketh uprightly walketh securely; but he that perverteth his ways shall be known" [Prov. 10:9]. "He that walketh uprightly," he said; that is, the man who goes in the path of the Torah, and such a man "walketh securely," and the evil forces in the world can render him no harm; but "he that perverteth his ways" and wanders from the path of truth "shall be known," in this wise, that he shall be marked out for those appointed to sit in judgment, who will keep his image in mind until such time as they will lead him to the selected place of judgment. But as for "him who walks in the way of truth," him God takes under his protection, so that the executioners of judgment cannot know him. Happy are they who walk in the way of truth.

THE GREAT FEAST

In a state of great sadness Rabbi Isaac one day sat down before Rabbi Judah's door. Coming out and seeing him thus, Rabbi Judah asked: What troubles you this day?

Rabbi Isaac replied: I have come to request three things of you. First, that whenever you recite any one of my elucidations of the Torah, you do so in my name. Second, I ask you to educate my son Joseph in Torah. And third, I ask that you go every seven days to my grave, and pray over it.

Rabbi Judah spoke: What cause have you to think you are going to die?

He answered: Of late my soul has been departing from

me in the night, and not illuminating me with dreams as was its wont. And, too, when I incline forward during prayer, I perceive that my shadow fails to show on the wall, and I surmise it is because the herald has gone forth and proclaimed regarding me.

Rabbi Judah then said: I will do as you ask. But in turn I ask you to keep a place for me by your side in the other world, to be together as in this.

Rabbi Isaac wept and answered: I beg you to stay by me for the rest of my days.

Together they went to Rabbi Simeon, who was engaged in study of the Torah. Rabbi Simeon raised his eyes, and saw Rabbi Isaac, and before him, running and dancing, the Angel of Death, and Rabbi Simeon walked to the door, and taking Rabbi Isaac by the hand, he said: I charge that he who is accustomed to enter shall enter, and he who is not shall not enter. Then Rabbi Isaac and Rabbi Judah entered and the Angel of Death was kept outside.

Looking at Rabbi Isaac, Rabbi Simeon perceived that his hour had not yet come, but that he had respite until the eighth hour of the day, and he made Rabbi Isaac sit down and study the Torah. Then said Rabbi Simeon to his son Rabbi Eleazar: Sit by the door, and do not speak to anyone, and if anyone should want to enter, on your oath say he may not.

He turned to Rabbi Isaac: Have you this day seen the face of your father? For we know that when the hour comes for a man to leave this world, he finds himself surrounded by his father and his relatives, and he looks at them and recognizes them, and sees all who were his companions in this world, and they escort his soul to the new abode it is to have.

To this Rabbi Isaac answered: I have not as yet seen.

Then Rabbi Simeon rose up and said: Master of the universe! Rabbi Isaac is illustrious among us, and one of the seven eyes of the world. I hold him, and therefore now give him to me.

Then a voice was heard: The throne of his Master is near the wings of Rabbi Simeon. Behold, he is yours and shall escort you when you go in to take abode on your throne.

Now Rabbi Eleazar beheld the Angel of Death approaching, and he said to him: Death cannot cast his doom in the place where Rabbi Simeon is.

Rabbi Simeon then called to his son: Come in here and support Rabbi Isaac, for I see that he is afraid.

This Rabbi Eleazar did, and Rabbi Simeon turned away to study. Now Rabbi Isaac fell asleep and in a dream he beheld his father, who said to him: My son, your lot is happy, in this world and in the world to come. For this reason, that among the leaves of the tree of life in the Garden of Eden stands a great tree, which is Rabbi Simeon ben Yohai, mighty in both worlds, and he shelters you with his branches.

Rabbi Isaac asked him: Father, what is my portion there?

He replied: Three days since, your chamber was roofed and made ready for you, with windows on all four sides to allow the light in, and when I saw your abode I was glad, and said: Your portion is a happy one; except that your son has still not learned enough of Torah. And see now, twelve righteous Companions desired greatly to visit you, and just as we were about to leave, a voice issued forth through all worlds, calling, Ye Companions that stand here, take pride in Rabbi Simeon, who has made a request and had it granted.* And more than that, there are here to be found seventy crowned places which are his, and each place has doors which open to seventy worlds, and each world opens to seventy channels and each channel is open to seventy supernal crowns, and thence are ways leading to the Ancient and Inscrutable One,† opening on a view of that celestial delight which gives bliss and illumination to all, as it is stated, "to see the pleasantness of the Lord and to visit His temple" [Ps. 27:4].

Then asked Rabbi Isaac: Father, how long is it given me to be in this world?

He replied: This I am not allowed to reveal, nor is it shown to a man. However, when the great feast of Rabbi Simeon‡ is held, thou shalt prepare his table.

Rabbi Isaac now awakened, and his face was smiling.

Observing this, Rabbi Simeon spoke: Have you not heard something?

Indeed, he replied; and related his dream, and prostrated himself before Rabbi Simeon.

From that day, it is told, Rabbi Isaac zealously taught the Torah to his son, whom he always kept by his side. When he went to converse with Rabbi Simeon, he used to

---

* That is, that Rabbi Isaac should live.
† God in his most hidden aspect.
‡ This feast is a parabolic expression for death.

leave his son outside, and sitting before Rabbi Simeon he applied to himself the words: "O Lord, I am oppressed, be Thou my surety" [Isa. 38:14].

We have learned that when a man's time arrives to leave the world, on that fearful day the four quarters of the world arraign him, and punishments come up from all four, and the four elements fall into dispute, each clamoring to depart to its own side. Whereupon a herald goes out and proclaims, and the proclamation is heard in two hundred and seventy worlds. If the man merit it, he is joyously welcomed by all the worlds, but if not, woe to the man and his portion!

We have learned that upon the herald's proclamation, a flame issues from the North, going through the "stream of fire" [Dan. 7:10], and splitting up to pass into the four quarters of the world, there to consume the souls of sinners. After which it leaves and shoots up and down till it settles between the wings of a black cock, which then flaps its wings and crows at the threshold of the gate. First it cries out: "For behold, the day cometh, it burneth as a furnace . . ." [Mal. 3:19]. The second time it cries: "For, lo, He that formeth the mountains, and createth the wind, and declareth unto man what is his thought" [Amos 4:13]; this is the time that a man's deeds bear witness against him and he admits them as his. The third time, they come to deprive him of his soul, and the cock calls: "Who would not fear Thee, O King of the nations? For it befitteth Thee" [Jer. 10:7].

Rabbi Yose said: Wherefore must it be a black cock?

Replied Rabbi Judah: A mystical meaning inheres in

whatever the Almighty does. We know that punishment falls only upon a place which is similar to it. Black being the symbol of the side of judgment, the flame, in going forth, lights on the wings of a black cock, which is the most fitting.

Thus it is when man's hour of judgment approaches, it starts to call to him; and only the sufferer himself knows, as we have learned, that a new spirit enters from above into a man lying ill, whose hour to depart from the world is near, and it is in virtue of this new spirit that he perceives what he could not before perceive, and then he goes from the world. Thus it is written: "For man shall not see Me and live" [Exod. 33:20]; in lifetime, no, but at the hour of death, it is permitted.

We saw, moreover, that a man, in the hour of his death, is permitted to behold his relatives and companions from the other world. All these rejoice before him, and greet him if he is righteous, but if not, then only the sinners who are daily thrust down into Gehinnom recognize him. All are begloomed and "woe!" commences and ends their converse. Lifting up his eyes, he sees them as a flame darting from the fire, and he with them exclaims "woe!"

We have seen that when a man's soul leaves him, it is met by all his relatives and companions from the other world, who guide it to the realm of delight and the place of torture. If he is righteous, he beholds his place and ascends and is there installed and regaled with the delights of the other world. But if no, then his soul stays in this world until his body is buried in the earth, after which the executioners seize on him and drag him down to Dumah, the prince of Gehinnom, and to his allotted level in Gehinnom.

Rabbi Judah said: During seven days does the soul go from his house to his grave, and from his grave to his house, back and forth in mourning for the body, according to the verse: "But his flesh shall suffer pain for him, and his soul shall mourn over him" [Job 14:22], and as it beholds the grief of the house, it also grieves.

Now we know that at the end of the seven days the decay of the body sets in, and the soul then goes in to its place. It is first permitted into the cave of Machpelah up to a point, set in accordance with its merit. Then it comes to where the Garden of Eden stands, and there encounters the cherubim and the flashing sword which is found in the lower Garden of Eden, and if it is deemed worthy to do so, it enters.

We know that there four pillars are waiting, and in their hands they hold the form of a body which the soul joyfully dons as its garment, and then it abides in its allotted circle of the Lower Garden for the stated time. After that a herald issues proclamation and there is brought out a pillar of three hues, called "the habitation of mount Zion" [Isa. 4:5]. By this pillar the soul ascends to the gate of righteousness, where are to be found Zion and Jerusalem. Happy is the lot of the soul deemed worthy to ascend higher, for then it is together with the Body of the King. If it does not merit to ascend higher, then "he that is left in Zion, and he that remaineth in Jerusalem, shall be called holy" [Isa. 4:3]. But when a soul is granted to ascend higher, then it sees before it the glory of the King, and is vouchsafed the supernal delight from the region which is called Heaven. He upon whom this grace is bestowed, fortunate is he.

Rabbi Yose said: There is a higher grace and a lower grace. The higher grace is found above the heavens, as it stands written: "For Thy mercy is great *above* the heavens" [Ps. 108:5]. And concerning the lower grace it says: "For Thy mercy is great *unto* the heavens" [Ps. 57:11], and of this latter are the "faithful mercies of David" [Isa. 55:3].

"And the days drew near that Israel must die" [Gen. 47: 29].

Rabbi Hiyya said: Here, in the mention of his death, the name Israel is written, while above, in speaking of his life, he is called Jacob, as it is written, "And Jacob lived . . ." [Gen. 47:28]. Why is this? Rabbi Yose replied: Remark now the word "days." Is it not strange, for a man dies only on one day, or rather, in one instant.

The reason, however, is this: When God has decided to receive back a man's spirit, he passes in review all the days of the man's life in this world. And happy the man whose days draw near to pass before the King without blame, with not a single one rejected on account of any sin therein. Thus, "draw near" is said of the righteous, inasmuch as their days draw near to pass before the King without blame. And woe unto the wicked, whose days were all spent in sin and go unrecorded above, and hence their days cannot draw near. Of them it says: "The way of the wicked is as darkness; they know not at what they stumble" [Prov. 4:19].

Therefore it is written that the days of Israel "drew near," without blame and with unblemished joy; therefore is the name Israel used, to signify a greater perfection than the name Jacob.

Said Rabbi Yose: There are certain righteous ones whose days, when they are reckoned up, are placed away from the King, and others are there whose days are brought near to the King, and their portion is blessed, and among these was Israel.

"And he called his son Joseph" [Gen. 47:29]. Were, then, the other ones not his sons?

Rabbi Abba explained: We see that Joseph is spoken of as Jacob's son in a more poignant way than his brethren. For, we remember that when he was tempted by Potiphar's wife, he looked up and beheld his father's image (as it is written, "and there was none of the men of the house there within" [Gen. 39:11], which we take to mean, "but there was someone else"), and when Joseph saw his father, he resisted and left. And so Jacob, when blessing all his sons, said to Joseph: "I know it, my son, I know it" [Gen. 48:19], and in the repetition of the word is meant: I know the occasion when in your very body you proved you were my son.

Also, it is explained that Joseph so nearly resembled his father that whoever saw him recognized he was the son of Jacob. Therefore did Jacob say to him "my son." To this Rabbi Yose added another reason, namely, that Joseph was the mainstay of Jacob and his family in Jacob's old age.

Moreover, Jacob requested Joseph and not any other son to bury him, for Joseph alone could take him out of Egypt.

Rabbi Yose then asked: Jacob knew that his descendants would be slaves in Egypt; why then did he not show the true concern of a parent and cause himself to be buried there, so that his merit might shield them? However, we know through tradition that Jacob, when he was ready to go into Egypt, was beset with the fear that his posterity might be lost among the nations and that God might withdraw his Presence from him. And therefore God said to him: "Fear not to go down into Egypt, for I will there make of thee a great nation" [Gen. 46:3], and further, "I will go down with thee into Egypt" [Gen. 46:4]. Still Jacob feared that he might be buried in Egypt and not with his ancestors, whereupon God said: "I will also surely bring thee up again" [*ibid.*], which is to say, so that you may be buried with your fathers.

Thus, for several reasons Jacob wished to be returned from Egypt. For one, because he had knowledge that God would punish the gods of the Egyptians, and he feared lest the Egyptians should make a god of him. Also, he was certain that God would not withdraw his Presence from among his descendants in exile. Third, he desired that his body be laid to rest together with his ancestors, so as to be among them and not with the sinners of Egypt, for Jacob, as we know, repeated the beauty of Adam, and was of a form sublime and holy, like to the holy throne. The secret of the matter is, however, that there is no separation among the patriarchs, and therefore he said: "when I sleep with my fathers" [Gen. 47:30].

Still another reason that Jacob addressed Joseph as "my son": it was to Rachel that Jacob had given his whole devotion, and from the very beginning he had been more eager to beget Joseph than any other of the sons.

Rabbi Simeon said: All man's acts are written down in a book, and scrutinized by the holy King and stand revealed before him; therefore let man take grave concern neither to sin nor in any way to go against the will of his Master, for even man's thoughts are known to God and do not elude him.

The night when Jacob went in to Leah and she offered him the tokens he had provided Rachel with, he was led to believe she was Rachel, and God from whom no secret is hidden permitted Jacob's thought to hold, and thus the birthright of Reuben was given over to Joseph, it having been Jacob's first seed, and so Rachel came into her own inheritance. Therefore it is that Leah named him Reuben [see a son] and not Reubeni [see my son].

We have been taught: God was aware that Jacob had not the intention to transgress before him, nor did he allow his mind to turn to any other woman at that moment as do the sinful, and therefore it is written: "Now the sons of Jacob were twelve" [Gen. 35:22]. There is another name known to the Companions for the son begotten by a sinner who acts thus. Therefore it is said, Jacob "called his son Joseph"—his very son, his son in the first and at the last.

"Put, I pray thee, thy hand under my thigh" [Gen. 47: 29].

Rabbi Yose said: Jacob insisted he swear by the mark of the covenant which had been put into his flesh, for this was held by the patriarchs to be paramount, and this covenant is also symbolized by Joseph.

Rabbi Simeon said: We find the same, "put thy hand under my thigh," with reference to Abraham and to Jacob both, but not in connection with Isaac, for the reason that Esau came out of Isaac.

Further, it may be imagined that Jacob meant: Swear to me by the holy mark which has yielded into the world holy and faithful seed, remaining always undefiled, that

you will not bury me among the unclean ones who have
taken no heed to it.—If so, why, one may ask, was Joseph,
who kept the covenant, buried among them? On this account: for the sake of a particular situation, as when God
appeared to Ezekiel outside the Holy Land, by the river
Chebar. For God saw that were Joseph to be taken away,
the Israelites would be stamped down in bondage, and so
he said: Make his burial in the water,* a place which is
not susceptible of [levitical] uncleanness, and then the
Israelites will be enabled to endure the captivity.

Rabbi Yose said: Jacob perceived that, like his fathers,
he was in all ways suited to become part of the holy chariot
[on which the Divinity rests], but he deemed it impossible
for his body to be conjoined to his fathers if he were buried
in Egypt.

The patriarchs, as is known, were permitted to have
their wives buried with them in the cave of Machpelah,
and why then was Jacob buried with Leah, and not with
Rachel, who was the "foundation of the house"? On this
account, that Leah bore more children from the holy seed.

Rabbi Judah said: When Leah heard that Jacob was
righteous, she used to go out each day to the highway and
weep for him and pray for him. Rachel never did this.
Wherefore it was granted Leah to be buried with him, but
Rachel's grave was set by the highway.

In secret doctrine, as we have established, the reason is
that the one symbolizes the revealed, the other the hidden
sphere of being. We know from tradition that the virtu-

---

* According to tradition, Joseph's coffin was placed in the river,
where it remained until the Exodus.

ous Leah shed much tears praying that she be given to Jacob and not to the wicked Esau. And thus we perceive that whoever has a punishment marked out for him can effect that it be cancelled by praying with tears before the Almighty; so Leah, assigned to Esau by divine decree, yet managed by prayer to satisfy her preference for Jacob and kept herself from being given to Esau.

Rabbi Isaac said: It stands written, "And Solomon's wisdom excelled the wisdom of all the children of the east" [I Kings 5:10]. What is meant by the wisdom of the children of the East? We know from tradition that this was the wisdom inherited by them from Abraham. For we read that Abraham "gave all that he had unto Isaac" [Gen. 25:5]; by this is meant the higher wisdom, which was Abraham's because he possessed the knowledge of the holy name of God. "But to the sons of the concubines, that Abraham had, Abraham gave gifts" [Gen. 25:6], that is, knowledge of a kind about the lower crowns [the demonic forces], and he established them in the "east country" [*ibid.*], and it was from this source that the children of the East received their magic wisdom. . . .

"But when I sleep with my fathers" [Gen. 47:30].

Happy is the portion of the patriarchs: they are made a holy chariot for God, who has found delight in them and been crowned with them; therefore is it written, "Only the Lord had a delight in thy fathers" [Deut. 10:15].

Rabbi Eleazar said: Jacob had knowledge that he would be crowned in his fathers and his fathers with him. . . .

Rabbi Judah said: Men's ears are shut to the admonitions of the Torah, and their eyes to their own state, in not realizing that in the day on which a human being appears in the world there appear all the days assigned to him, and these swarm about the world and then each in turn descends to the man to warn him. And if the man, being so warned, yet transgresses against his Master, then that day in which he transgressed ascends in shame and stands isolated outside, bearing witness, and remains thus until the man repents. If the man turns to righteousness, the day goes back to its position, but if not, then it goes to join the outer spirit and returns to its dwelling and then takes on the very same shape as the man, so as to plague him, and it stays with him in his house. If the man prove righteous, it proves a good companion; if not, it is an evil companion. Either way, this kind of day is missing from the full number and not reckoned in with the others.

Woe to the man that has lessened his days before the Almighty, nor left himself days wherewith to crown himself in the other world and to draw near to the holy King. For being worthy, he ascends by virtue of those days, and those days in which he did righteously and sinned not become for his soul a garment of splendor. Woe to him that has lessened his days above, for the days damaged by his sins are lacking when it comes time to be garbed in his days, and his garment is therefore imperfect; worse is it if there are many such, and then he has nothing at all for garb in the other world. Alas for him and for his soul: he is punished in Gehinnom many days for each of those days, seeing that when he left this world he was without any days to be garbed in, he had no garment to put over him.

The righteous are the happy ones, for their days are in store with the holy King, and make a splendid attire for clothing themselves in, in the other world. This is the secret meaning of the verse, "and they knew that they were naked" [Gen. 3:7], which is to say, the glorious vestments composed of those days had been ruined and no day was left to be clothed in. It remained so until Adam repented. Then God pardoned him and made other clothes for him, but these were not made from his days, as it stands: "And the Lord God made for Adam and for his wife garments of skins, and clothed them" [Gen. 3:21].

We see that concerning Abraham it says "he came into days" [Gen. 24:1], for on leaving this world he did indeed gain possession of his previous days as an investiture, and his garment of splendor was abundant and perfect. But Job said of himself: "Naked came I out of my mother's womb, and naked shall I return thither" [Job 1:21], inasmuch as there was no garment left with which to clothe himself.

Our teachers have taught: The righteous are glad, forasmuch as their days are without blemish and stay for the world to come, and so, after death, the days are put together to make a garment of splendor in which they have the honor to taste of the delights of the future world, and in which they are destined to receive life again. But woe to the sinners whose days are damaged and in consequence nothing is left with which to clothe themselves when they depart from the world.

Moreover, we have learned that all they who by righteousness have gained for themselves a garment of glory made of their days are in the future world crowned like the patriarchs, with crowns from the stream that flows unceasing into the Garden of Eden, and it is written of these: "The Lord will guide thee continually, and satisfy thy soul in resplendent places" [Isa. 58:11], but the sinners who have failed to get themselves such a garment will be "like a tamarisk in the desert, and shall not see when good cometh; but shall inhabit the parched places in the wilderness" [Jer. 17:6].

Rabbi Isaac then said: Jacob, of all men, had the happiest chance, for the garment was his due by virtue both of his days and those of his ancestors; therefore he said: "when I sleep with my fathers."

Rabbi Judah said: When Jacob went in to obtain the blessing from his father, he was clothed in the clothes of Esau, yet it is written that Isaac smelled *his* raiment [Gen. 27:27], that is, there came to his nostrils the odor of Jacob's raiment in the future world, and it was on this account he blessed him. And so he said: "See, the smell of my son is as the smell of a field which the Lord hath blessed" [*ibid.*], which refers to the field of holy apple trees wherein dew from the realm called heaven drops each day; and he continued: "So God give thee of the dew of heaven" [Gen. 27:28]. We have been taught that every day from the Garden of Eden there rise fifteen odors with which are perfumed the precious raiment in the other world.

Rabbi Judah inquired as to how many garments there are. Rabbi Eleazar replied: On this point, the masters differ, but actually, there are three. One is to clothe the spirit [*ruaḥ*] in the earthly Garden of Eden. Most precious is the second, which is for the clothing of the innermost soul [*neshamah*] when it is among the "bundle of life" [I Sam. 25:29] in the circle of the King. The third is an outer cloak, appearing and disappearing, with which the vital soul [*nefesh*] is clothed. This one moves around from place to place in this world and on the Sabbaths and the New Moons it seeks out the spirit in the earthly paradise, from which it learns certain things and the knowledge of these it spreads in this world. It is taught that on Sabbaths and New Moons the soul [*nefesh*] pays two visits. First, it seeks out the spirit, among the perfumes of the earthly paradise, and then together with the spirit it seeks out the higher soul in the "bundle of life," and regales itself on the splendid radiance emanating from both sides. This is implied in the words, "The Lord will . . . satisfy thy soul in resplendent places" [Isa. 58:11], where the plural is meant to include the two, the outer refulgence of the place of the spirit, and the radiance within radiance which comes to them by being with the higher soul in the "bundle of life."

On a certain occasion, wishing to get away from the heat of the sun, Rabbi Eleazar and Rabbi Abba turned into a cave at Lydda. Rabbi Abba spoke: Let us now compass this cave about with words of the Torah. Rabbi Eleazar then began, quoting the verse: "Set me as a seal upon thy heart, as a seal upon thine arm . . . the flashes thereof are flashes of fire, a very flame of the Lord" [Cant. 8:6].

He said: This verse has provoked great discussion. One night I was in attendance on my father, and I heard him say that it is the souls of the righteous, they alone, which effect the true devotion of the Community of Israel to God, and her longing for him, for these souls make possible the flow of the lower waters toward the upper, and this brings about perfect friendship and the yearning for mutual embrace in order to bring forth fruit. When they cleave one to the other, then says the Community of Israel in the largeness of her affection: "Set me as a seal upon thy heart." For, as the imprint of the seal is to be discerned even after the seal is withdrawn, so I shall cling to you, even after I am taken from you and enter into captivity: thus says the Community of Israel.

Thus, "Set me as a seal upon thy heart," so that I may remain upon you in semblance, as the imprint of a seal.

"For love is strong as death" [*ibid.*], violent, as is the separation of the spirit from the body; for we have learned that when a man is come to leave this world and he sees wondrous things, his spirit, like an oarless boatman tossing up and down and making no headway on the sea, also

tosses up and down through his limbs, asking leave of each
one; and only with great rending is its separation performed. Thus, violently, does the Community of Israel
love God. "Jealousy is cruel as the grave" [*ibid.*]. Without jealousy, it is not true love. Thus we learn that for a
man's love of his wife to be perfect, he should be jealous,
for then he will not look after any other woman.

As they sat, they heard Rabbi Simeon approaching on
the road, with Rabbi Judah and Rabbi Isaac. When Rabbi
Simeon came to the cave, Rabbi Eleazar and Rabbi Abba
emerged from it. Said Rabbi Simeon: From the walls of
the cave I perceive that the Divine Presence hovers here.
And they all sat down.

Rabbi Simeon asked: What have you been discoursing
of?

Rabbi Abba replied: Of the love that the Community of
Israel bears to God. And Rabbi Eleazar cited in that connection the words: "Set me as a seal upon thy heart."

Rabbi Simeon said: Eleazar, it was the celestial love and
the ties of affection which you were in the act of perceiv-
ing. Then he remained silent for a time, and at last said:
Always silence is agreeable, save where the Torah is concerned. I possess a jewel which I would share with you.
It is a profound idea which I came upon in the book of
Rav Hamnuna the Elder. It is this:

Always, it is the male who pursues the female seeking
to stimulate her love, but in this case we see the female
pursuing the male and paying court, a thing not ordinarily
accounted fitting for the female. But in this there is a
profound mystery, one of the most cherished treasures of

the King. We know that three souls pertain to the divine grades. Nay, four, for there is one supernal soul which is unperceivable, certainly to the keeper of the lower treasury, and even to that of the upper. This is the soul of all souls, incognizable and inscrutable. All is contingent on it, which is veiled in a dazzling bright veil. From it are formed pearls which are tissued together like the joints of the body, and these it enters into, and through them manifests its energy. It and they are one, there being no division between them. Yet another, a female soul, is concealed amidst her hosts and has a body adhering to her through which she manifests her power, as the soul in the human body.

These souls are as copies of the hidden joints above. Yet another soul is there, namely, the souls of the righteous below, which, coming from the higher souls, the soul of the female and the soul of the male, are hence preeminent above all the heavenly hosts and camps. It may be wondered, if they are thus preëminent on both sides, why do they descend to this world only to be taken thence at some future time?

This may be explained by way of a simile: A king has a son whom he sends to a village to be educated until he shall have been initiated into the ways of the palace. When the king is informed that his son is now come to maturity, the king, out of his love, sends the matron his mother to bring him back into the palace, and there the king rejoices with him every day. In this wise, the Holy One, be blessed, possessed a son from the Matron, that is, the supernal holy soul. He despatched it to a village, that is, to this world, to be raised in it, and initiated into the ways of the King's palace. Informed that his son was now come to maturity, and should be returned to the palace, the King, out of love, sent the Matron for him to bring him into the palace. The soul does not leave this world until such time as the Matron has arrived to get her and bring her into the King's palace, where she abides for ever. Withal, the village people weep for the departure of the king's son from among them. But one wise man said to them: Why do you weep? Was this not the king's son, whose true place is in his father's palace, and not with you? . . .

If the righteous were only aware of this, they would be filled with joy when their time comes to leave this world. For does it not honor them greatly that the Matron comes down on their account, to take them into the King's palace, where the King may every day rejoice in them? For to God there is no joy save in the souls of the righteous. Only the souls of the righteous here on earth can stir the love of the Community of Israel for God, for they come from the King's side, the side of the male. This transport goes on to the female and excites her love, and thus does the male stir the love and fondness of the female, and the female is united with the male in love. In like manner the female's desire to pour forth lower waters to mingle with the upper waters* is incited only through the souls of the right-

* The upper and the lower waters represent the "male" and the "female" forces, or active and passive principles in creation.

eous. And so, happy are the righteous in this world and the world to come, for on them the upper and lower beings are based. Hence it stands written: "The righteous is the foundation of the world" [Prov. 10:25].

EXODUS

If one should ask: Is it not written, "For ye saw no manner of similitude" [Deut. 4:15], the answer would be: Truly, it was granted us to behold him in a given similitude, for concerning Moses it is written, "and the similitude of the Lord doth he behold" [Num. 12:8]. Yet the Lord was revealed only in that similitude which Moses saw, and in none other, of any creation formed by His signs. Therefore it stands written: "To whom then will ye liken God? Or what likeness will ye compare unto Him?" [Isa. 40:18]. Also, even that similitude was a semblance of the Holy One, be blessed, not as he is in his very place which we know to be impenetrable, but as the King manifesting his might of dominion over his entire creation, and thus appearing to each one of his creatures as each can grasp him, as it is written: "And by the ministry of the prophets have I used similitudes" [Hos. 12:11].* Hence says He: Albeit in your own likeness do I represent myself, to whom will you compare me and make me comparable?

Because in the beginning, shape and form having not yet been created, He had neither form nor similitude. Hence is it forbidden to one apprehending him as he is before Creation to imagine him under any kind of form or shape, not even by his letters *hé* and *vav*,† not either by

---

* This verse is taken to mean that God manifests himself to each prophet according to his capacity of grasping God.
† The four letters of the holy name YHVH are understood as symbols of the manifestations of God's creative power in every being.

his complete holy Name, nor by letter or sign of any kind. Thus, "For ye saw no manner of similitude" means, You beheld nothing which could be imagined in form or shape, nothing which you could embody into a finite conception.

But when He had created the shape of supernal man, it was to him for a chariot, and on it he descended, to be known by the appellation YHVH, so as to be apprehended by his attributes and in each particular one, to be perceived. Hence it was he caused himself to be named *El, Elohim, Shaddai, Zevaot* and YHVH, of which each was a symbol among men of his several divine attributes, making manifest that the world is upheld by mercy and justice, in accordance with man's deeds. If the radiance of the glory of the Holy One, be blessed, had not been shed over his entire creation, how could even the wise have apprehended him? He would have continued to be unknowable, and the words could not be verily said, "The whole earth is full of His glory" [Isa. 6:3].

However, woe to the man who should make bold to identify the Lord with any single attribute, even if it be His own, and the less so any human form existent, "whose foundation is in the dust" [Job 4:19], and whose creatures are frail, soon gone, soon lost to mind. Man dare project one sole conception of the Holy One, be blessed, that of his sovereignty over some one attribute or over the creation in its entirety. But if he be not seen under these manifestations, then there is neither attribute, nor likeness, nor form in him; as the very sea, whose waters lack form and solidity in themselves, having these only when they are spread over the vessel of the earth.

From this we may reckon it so: One, is the source of the sea. A current comes forth from it making a revolution which is *yod*.* The source is one, and the current makes two. Then is formed the vast basin known as the sea, which is like a channel dug into the earth, and it is filled by the waters issuing from the source; and this sea is the third thing. This vast basin is divided up into seven channels, resembling that number of long tubes, and the waters go from the sea into the seven channels. Together, the source, the current, the sea, and the seven channels make the number ten. If the Creator who made these tubes should choose to break them, then would the waters return to their source, and only broken vessels would remain, dry, without water.

In this same wise has the Cause of causes derived the ten aspects of his Being which are known as *sefirot,* and named the crown the Source, which is a never-to-be-exhausted fountain of light, wherefrom he designates himself *eyn sof,* the Infinite. Neither shape nor form has he, and no vessel exists to contain him, nor any means to apprehend him. This is referred to in the words: "Refrain from searching after the things that are too hard for thee, and refrain from seeking for the thing which is hidden from thee."†

Then He shaped a vessel diminutive as the letter *yod,* and filled it from him, and called it Wisdom-gushing

---

* The first letter in the name of God.
† Ben Sira, as quoted in the Talmud, Hagigah 13a.

Fountain, and called himself wise on its account. And after, he fashioned a large vessel named sea, and designated it Understanding [*binah*] and himself understanding, on its account. Both wise and understanding is he, in his own essence; whereas Wisdom in itself cannot claim that title, but only through him who is wise and has made it full from his fountain; and so Understanding in itself cannot claim that title, but only through him who filled it from his own essence, and it would be rendered into an aridity if he were to go from it. In this regard, it is written, "As the waters fail from the sea, and the river is drained dry" [Job 14:11].

Finally, "He smites [the sea] into seven streams" [Isa. 11:15], that is, he directs it into seven precious vessels, the which he calls Greatness, Strength, Glory, Victory, Majesty, Foundation, Sovereignty;* in each he designates himself thus: great in Greatness, strong in Strength, glorious in Glory, victorious in Victory, "the beauty of our Maker" in Majesty, righteous in Foundation [cf. Prov. 10: 25]. All things, all vessels, and all worlds does he uphold in Foundation.

In the last, in Sovereignty, he calls himself King, and his is "the greatness, and the strength, and the glory, and the victory, and the majesty; for all that is in heaven and in the earth is Thine; Thine is the kingdom, O Lord, and Thou art exalted as head above all" [I Chron. 29:11]. In his power lie all things, be it that he chooses to reduce the number of vessels, or to increase the light issuing therefrom, or be it the contrary. But over him, there exists no

---

* These designate the seven lower *sefirot*.

deity with power to increase or reduce.

Also, he made beings to serve these vessels: each a throne supported by four columns, with six steps to the throne; in all, ten. Altogether, the throne is like the cup of benediction about which ten statements are made [in the Talmud], harmonious with the Torah which was given in Ten Words [the Decalogue], and with the Ten Words by which the world was created.

OUT OF THE DEPTHS

"Out of the depths have I called unto thee, O Lord" [Ps. 130:1, 2]. Because it stands without name of author, all men of all generations can take this Psalm for their very own. It is incumbent on any man praying before the holy King to pray from the depths of his soul, for then will his heart be entirely directed to God and his mind entirely bent on his prayer.

David had already said, "With my whole heart have I sought thee" [Ps. 119:10]. Why, we may ask, need he go beyond this, and say "out of the depths"? It is on this account, that a man must needs give his mind and heart exclusively to the thought of the source of all sources when he prays before the King, so that he may draw up benedictions from [the spheres called] "the depth of the well," the source of all life, the "stream coming out of Eden" [Gen. 2:10], which "maketh glad the city of God" [Ps. 46:5].

Prayer is the drawing of this blessing from above to below:* when the Ancient One, the All-hidden, desires to bless the world, he causes to come together in the heavenly depth his bounties of grace, from where human prayer will draw them into the "well," thereby making it possible for all the streams and brooks to be filled.

TWO ASPECTS

Rabbi Abba spoke: What did the Israelites mean by saying: "Is the Lord among us, or not?" [*ayin*, nothing; Exod. 17:7]. Could it be that in their folly they were unaware he was among them? Were they not encircled by the Divine Presence and surrounded by clouds of glory? Did they not, by the sea, behold the light of the refulgent majesty of their King? Have we not heard it said that a serving maid at the Red Sea was vouchsafed greater vision than Ezekiel?

The explanation is, as Rabbi Simeon has made it, that the Israelites wished to ascertain whether the manifestation of the Divine which they had been given was of the Ancient One, the All-hidden One, the Transcendent, who, being above comprehension, is designated *ayin* [nothing], or whether of the "Small Countenance," the Immanent, which is designated YHVH. Therefore for the word *lo*

* The Zohar takes the verse to mean: "Out of the depths [in which thou art] I call thee up."

[not] we have here the word *ayin* [nothing].

One may ask, why then were the Israelites chastised? The reason is they made distinction between these two aspects in God, and "tried the Lord" [*ibid.*], saying to themselves: We shall pray in one way, if it is the One, and in another way if it is the Other.

SABBATH

"Remember the sabbath day, to keep it holy" [Exod. 20: 8].

Rabbi Isaac said: It stands written: "And God blessed the seventh day" [Gen. 2: 3]; notwithstanding, it is said of the manna, "Six days ye shall gather it, but on the seventh day is the sabbath, in it there shall be none" [Exod. 16: 26]. What blessing can that day carry which was lacking in food? Still, we have learned that from the seventh day accrue all blessings above and below. Why was just this day, therefore, lacking in manna?

It is explained thus: the six "days" of the transcendent world derive their blessings from the seventh day, and out of that which it received from the seventh day, each of the six supernal days sends forth food to the world below. Hence, whosoever has attained to the grade of faith, it is incumbent on him to make ready a table and a meal on the Sabbath eve [Friday] in order that his table be blessed throughout the remaining six days of the week. This is so because together with the Sabbath preparation, there is prepared the blessing for the full six days to come, inasmuch as an empty table holds no blessing. Hence one should provide the table with bread and other food on the Sabbath eve.

Rabbi Isaac added: And as well on the Sabbath day.

Rabbi Judah said: On this day one must needs celebrate three meals so that the day may refresh and satisfy.

Rabbi Abba said: This one must do, so that the supernal days which derive their blessing from the seventh may themselves be blessed. On this day does the dew which comes down from the Holy Ancient One, the All-hidden One,* fill the head of the "Small Countenance"; he makes it to descend into the holy "Field of Apple Trees"† three times after the coming in of the Sabbath, so that all may in union enjoy the blessing. From this it follows that the three meals of the day are necessary not for ourselves alone, but for all creation, for in such wise is fulfilled the true faith in the Holy Ancient One, the "Small Countenance," and the "Field of Apple Trees," and in all three we should take joy and delight. And it is as if he mars and breaks the perfection of the regions above, who fails to partake of all three repasts. . . .

Because the Sabbath is the center of the faith, therefore is man endowed on this day with an added, supernal soul, in which is all perfection, in accordance with the design of the world to come. What is the meaning of the word

* See the passage, Two Aspects.
† "Field of Apple Trees" symbolizes the sphere of the Divine Presence.

Sabbath? The Name of the Holy One, be blessed, the Name of perfect harmony on all sides.

Said Rabbi Yose: In truth, it is so. Alas for him who aids not in perfecting the joy of the holy King! What then is that joy? The three meals of the Faith, the meals whereof Abraham, Isaac and Jacob partake, and through which joy upon joy is expressed, the perfect faith from all sides. As we have been taught, on this day the fathers are crowned and all the children are inspired with power and light and joy, to an extent not given even on other festal days. Sinners get respite in Gehinnom on this day. Punishment is withheld from the world on this day. On this day the Torah is crowned in crowns of perfection. On this day joy and gladness reverberate throughout two hundred and fifty worlds. This, too, observe. On each of the six days of the week, at the hour of the afternoon prayer, the force prevails of unmitigated judgment, and retribution stands by. Not so on the Sabbath. When the hour of the Sabbath afternoon prayer has come, regnant are the benign influences, the lovingkindness of the Holy Ancient One is made manifest, all punishments are restrained, and joy and satisfaction are everywhere. In this hour of satisfaction and grace, the holy, faithful prophet Moses departed from this world, so that it might be known that he was not taken away through judgment, but that his soul ascended in the hour of grace of the Holy Ancient One, to be hidden in him. Hence, "No man knoweth of his sepulchre unto this day" [Deut. 34:6]. Thus, as the Holy Ancient One is the All-hidden, unknowable to those above and those below, so also was the soul of Moses hidden, in the revelation, at the Sabbath afternoon prayer, of God's grace. Of all hidden things in the world, this soul of Moses is the most hidden, and cannot come under judgment. Blessed is the portion of Moses.

On this day is the Torah crowned in perfect glory, in all its commandments, in all the decrees, in all the chastisements of transgression: a crown of seventy branches of light radiating on all sides. O, to see the little twigs shooting forth from each branch, and five of the branches stand in the Tree itself, where all branches are comprised! O, to behold the gates opening on all sides, streaming forth the splendor and glory of inexhaustible light! A voice is heard: Awake, you heavenly saints! Awake, holy people, chosen above, and chosen below! In gladness awake to meet your Lord, in perfect gladness awake! Make ready, in the threefold joy of the three patriarchs! Make ready for the Faith, joy of joys! O Israelites, how you are happy, holy in this world, holy in the world to come! Beyond all heathen nations, this is your inheritance—"a sign between Me and you" [Exod. 31:13].

Said Rabbi Judah: It is so, in truth. Hence: "Remember the sabbath day to keep it holy"; "Ye shall be holy, for I the Lord your God am holy" [Lev. 19:2]; "Call the sabbath a delight, and the holy of the Lord, honourable" [Isa. 58:13].

One night, Rabbi Hiyya and Rabbi Yose met together at the tower of Tyre, and were indeed happy to have each other for companion.

Said Rabbi Yose: How good it is to look upon the face of the Divine Presence! All the time I was on my way here, I had to suffer the annoying chatter of the old man who drove the donkey. He bothered me with every kind of foolish question; for example, What serpent flies in the air with an ant lying quietly between its teeth? What commences in union and ends up in separation? What eagle has its nest in a tree that does not exist and its young plundered by creatures not yet created, in a place which is not? What are they who descend when they ascend, and ascend when they descend? What is it of which two are one and one is three? Who is the beautiful virgin who has no eyes?* and a body concealed, yet revealed—concealed in the daytime, revealed in the morning?—and is bedecked with ornaments which are not? This is the manner in which he kept pestering me the whole journey. But at last I can enjoy peace and quiet, and we can give ourselves to discussion of Torah instead of to time wasted in silly chatter.

Rabbi Hiyya said: Dost thou know the old man at all?

Rabbi Yose replied: I know this, that he has nothing in him; if he had, he would have dwelled on some words of Scripture, and we would not have simply wasted the time

* The phrase could also be taken to mean: on whom nobody has set eyes. The following passage understands it so.

on the road.

Rabbi Hiyya then asked: Is the old man in this house? For it may chance at times that a seemingly hollow vessel holds some grains of gold.

Rabbi Yose replied: Yes, he is here, he is getting fodder ready for the donkey.

Whereupon they summoned him, and he came. The old man immediately uttered this: Now the two have turned into three, and the three into one! Said Rabbi Yose: I told you, did I not, that he is forever uttering nonsense? The old man sat down, and said: Sirs, only lately have I taken to driving a donkey. I have a young son who goes to school, and I should like to raise him in the study of the Torah; that is why, whenever I spot a scholar along my way, I go after him, hoping to learn something new in connection with the Torah; but today I have learned nothing new.

Rabbi Yose spoke: One thing especially, of all that I heard you say, amazed me, it showed so great foolishness in a man of your years, unless you did not know what you were talking about.

The old man said: What are you referring to?

Rabbi Yose replied: What you said concerning the beautiful virgin and the rest. . . .

At this point in his discourse [on the paradoxes], the old man paused, and then the two rabbis fell down before him, and weeping they said: Had we entered this world just to be able to listen to these words of yours from your mouth, it would have been enough.

Said he: Companions, it was not just to say what I have said up to now that I entered upon this discourse with you, for certainly an old man such as I would hardly stop at one utterance, making a sound like a single coin in a jar. What a multitude of humans there are who dwell in confusion, failing to perceive the way of truth that abides in the Torah, and the Torah, in love, summons them day after day to her, but woe, they do not so much as turn their heads. It is just as I have stated, the Torah releases one word, and comes forth from her sheath ever so little, and then retreats to concealment again. But this she does only for them who understand her and follow her precepts.

She may be compared to a beautiful and stately maiden, who is secluded in an isolated chamber of a palace, and has a lover of whose existence she alone knows. For love of her he passes by her gate unceasingly, and turns his eyes in all directions to discover her. She is aware that he is forever hovering about the palace, and what does she do? She thrusts open a small door in her secret chamber, for a moment reveals her face to her lover, then quickly withdraws it. He alone, none else, notices it; but he is aware it is from love of him that she has revealed herself to him for that moment, and his heart and his soul and everything within him are drawn to her.

So it is with the Torah, which discloses her innermost secrets only to them who love her. She knows that whosoever is wise in heart hovers near the gates of her dwelling place day after day. What does she do? From her palace, she shows her face to him, and gives him a signal of love, and forthwith retreats back to her hiding place. Only he alone catches her message, and he is drawn to her with his whole heart and soul, and with all of his being. In this manner, the Torah, for a moment, discloses herself in love to her lovers, so as to rouse them to renewed love. This then is the way of the Torah. In the beginning, when she first reveals herself to a man, she gives him some sign. If he understands, it is well, but if he fails, then she summons him and calls him "simpleton," and says to her messengers: Go tell that simpleton to come to me, and converse—as it is written: "Whoso is a simpleton, let him turn in hither" [Prov. 9:4]. And when he arrives, she commences to speak with him, at first from behind the veil which she has hung before her words, so that they may suit his manner of understanding, in order that he may progress gradually. This is known as *derashah*.* Then she speaks to him behind a filmy veil of finer mesh, she speaks to him in riddles and allegories—and these are called *haggadah*.

When, finally, he is on near terms with her, she stands disclosed face to face with him, and holds converse with him concerning all of her secret mysteries, and all the secret ways which have been hidden in her heart from immemorial time. Then is such a man a true adept in the Torah, a "master of the house," for to him she has uncovered all her mysteries, neither keeping back nor hiding any single one. She says to him: Do you see the sign, the cue, which I gave you in the beginning, how many mysteries it holds? He then comes to the realization that not one

* Derivation of the laws from the letter of the Scripture.

thing may be added to the words of the Torah, nor taken from them, not a sign and not a letter.

Hence should men pursue the Torah with all their might, so as to come to be her lovers, as we have shown.

THE DESTINY OF THE SOUL

At the time that the Holy One, be blessed, was about to create the world, he decided to fashion all the souls which would in due course be dealt out to the children of men, and each soul was formed into the exact outline of the body she was destined to tenant. Scrutinizing each, he saw that among them some would fall into evil ways in the world. Each one in its due time the Holy One, be blessed, bade come to him, and then said: Go now, descend into this and this place, into this and this body.

Yet often enough the soul would reply: Lord of the world, I am content to remain in this realm, and have no wish to depart to some other, where I shall be in thrall-dom, and become stained.

Whereupon the Holy One, be blessed, would reply: Thy destiny is, and has been from the day of thy forming, to go into that world.

Then the soul, realizing it could not disobey, would un-willingly descend and come into this world.

The Torah, counsel of the entire world, saw this, and cried to mankind: Behold, see how the Holy One, be blessed, takes pity on you! Without cost, he has sent to

you his costly pearl, that you may use it in this world, and
it is the holy soul.—"And if a man sell his daughter to be
a maid-servant" [Exod. 21:7], that is, when the Holy
One, be blessed, gives over to you his daughter the holy
soul for your maid servant, to be held in bondage by you,
I adjure you, in her due time, "she shall not go out as the
men-servants do" [*ibid.*], that is, stained with sin, but in
freedom, in light, in purity, so that her Master may rejoice
in her, and in rewarding her exceedingly with the glories
of Paradise, as it stands written: "And the Lord will . . .
satisfy thy soul with brightness" [Isa. 58:11], that is,
when she shall have ascended back to that sphere, bright
and pure.

But "if she please not her master" [Exod. 21:8], for
that she is fouled with sin, then woe to the body that has
eternally been deprived of its soul! The reason being, that
those souls which ascend from this world in a condition of
brightness and purity are put down in the King's archives,
each by name; and he says: Here is the soul of this certain
one; she appertains to the body which she left.—As it
stands written: "Who hath espoused her to himself"
[*ibid.*].

But "if she please not her master," which means, if she
be fouled by sin and guilt, he refuses to designate the same
body as before for her, and thus she is deprived of it for
ever, save if her Master grant her grace and lead her back
again to the body [by transmigration], for "then he let her
be redeemed" [*ibid.*], as it stands written: "He redeemeth
his soul from going into the pit" [Job 33:28]. This has
the meaning that man is counseled to redeem his soul by

his repentance. In truth, there is a twofold meaning in the words, "then he let her be redeemed," for they allude to a man's own redemption of his soul by repentance, and after it, the redemption from Gehinnom by the Holy One, be blessed.

"And if he espouse her unto his son, he shall deal with her after the manner of daughters" [Exod. 21:9]. How much heed should a man take lest he wander in a crooked path in this world! For if he shall have evidenced his worthiness in this world, having watched over his soul with every precaution, then the Holy One, be blessed, will be greatly content with him, and daily speak his praise before his supernal family, in this wise: See the holy son who is mine in that world below! Behold his deeds and the probity of his ways.

And when such a soul departs from this world, pure, bright, unblemished, the Holy One, be blessed, daily causes her to shine with a host of radiances and proclaims concerning her: Here is the soul of my son, such and such: let her be preserved for the body from which she has departed.

This is the significance of the words: "And if he espouse her unto his son, he shall deal with her after the manner of daughters." What mean the words, "after the manner of daughters"? It is a secret held solely in the trust of the wise: A palace which is known as the Palace of Love sits amidst a vast rock, a most secret firmament. Here in this place the treasures of the King are kept, and all his kisses of love. Every soul loved by the Holy One, be blessed, enters into that palace. And when the King makes his appearance, "Jacob kisses Rachel" [Gen. 29: 11], which is to say, the Lord discerns each holy soul, and taking each in turn to himself, embraces and fondles her, "dealing with her after the manner of daughters," even as a father acts toward his beloved daughter, embracing and fondling her, and presenting her with gifts.

SUFFERING OF INNOCENT CHILDREN

Solomon said: "But I returned and considered all the oppressed that are done [lit., made] under the sun; and behold the tears of such as were oppressed, and they had no comforter" [Eccles. 4:1].

Was he actually able to see all of those who were oppressed? Certainly not; but he was speaking of the infants who suckling at their mothers' breasts were taken away. Truly, the like of these are oppressed from every side, above in the celestial sphere, and oppressed below on earth. Most oppressed are the ones who are so on account of their inheritance, and of them it is written: "Visiting the iniquity of the fathers upon the children unto the third and fourth generation" [Exod. 20:5]. . . .

Consider the child born of the adulterous union of a man with his neighbor's wife, whom, openly or secretly, he has stolen; the Holy One, be blessed, is bound nevertheless to give a body and form to that child, and then truly is it "an oppressed one who is *made* such," that is, in spite of the Almighty. Reflecting on this matter, Solo-

mon said: I consider the grievous lot of these unfortunate
oppressed who have been "made," and the tears that they
weep before the Holy One, be blessed. Moaning, they put
their plaint to him: Surely, whoever sins, he must die.
But, King of the universe, a child aged but one day, shall
he be judged?—These are "the tears of such as were oppressed, and they had no comforter."

All shed tears, though among them are differences. One,
for instance, is a child conceived in incest. Immediately
upon issuing forth into the world, he is cut off from the
community of the holy people, and the unhappy bastard
weeps tears and wails before the Holy One, be blessed:
Lord of the world! If they who begot me did sin, what is
my guilt? For I have sought always to do only good works
before you.

But most grievous is the sorrow surrounding those "oppressed ones" who as still sucklings are taken from their
mothers' breasts. On their account, truly, the whole world
weeps; the tears that come from these babes have no equal,
their tears issue from the innermost and farthest places of
the heart, and the entire world is perplexed and says:
Eternally righteous are the judgments of the Holy One,
be blessed, and all his paths are paths of truth. Yet, is it
needful that these unhappy infants should die, who are
without sin and without blame? In this, where is the
rightful and just judgment of the Lord of the world? If
it is the parents' sins that are cause of their death, then
indeed they "had no comforter."

But, in reality, the tears shed by these "oppressed ones"
act as a petition and protection for the living, and by dint

of their innocence and the efficacy of their intercession, in time a place is prepared for them, such a one as cannot be attained to or occupied by even the most righteous; for the Holy One, be blessed, does in reality love these little ones with a unique and outstanding love. He unites them with himself and gets ready for them a place on high close by to him. And of these it is written: "Out of the mouth of babes and sucklings hast Thou founded strength" [Ps. 8:3].

THE THREE ASPECTS OF THE SOUL

The names and grades of the soul of man are three: *nefesh* [vital soul], *ruah* [spirit], *neshamah* [innermost soul, super-soul]. The three are comprehended one within the other, but each has its separate abode.

While the body in the grave is decomposing and moldering to dust, *nefesh* tarries with it, and it hovers about in this world, going here and there among the living, wanting to know their sorrows, and interceding for them at their need.

Ruah betakes itself into the earthly Garden of Eden. There, this spirit, desiring to enjoy the pleasures of the magnificent Garden, vests itself in a garment, as it were, of a likeness, a semblance of the body in which it had its abode in this world. On Sabbaths, New Moons and festival days, it ascends up to the supernal sphere, regaling itself with the delights there, and then it goes back to the Garden. As it is written: "And the spirit [*ruah*] returneth unto God who gave it" [Eccles. 12:7], that is, at the special holidays and times we have mentioned.

But *neshamah* ascends forthwith to her place, in the domain from which she emanated, and it is on her account that the light is lit, to shine above. Never thereafter does she descend to the earth. In *neshamah* is realized the One who embraces all sides, the upper and the lower. And until such time as *neshamah* has ascended to be joined with the Throne, *ruah* is unable to be crowned in the lower Garden and *nefesh* cannot rest easy in its place; but these find rest when she ascends.

Now when the children of men, being troubled and sorrowful, betake themselves to the graves of those who are gone, then *nefesh* is wakened, and it goes out to bestir *ruah,* which then rouses the patriarchs, and after, *neshamah.* Whereupon the Holy One, be blessed, has pity on the world. . . .

But if *neshamah* has for some reason been prevented from ascending to her proper place, then *ruah,* coming to the gate of the Garden of Eden, finds it closed against it, and, unable to enter, wanders about alone and dejected; while *nefesh,* too, flits from place to place in the world, and seeing the body in which it once was tenant eaten by worms and undergoing the judgment of the grave, it mourns for it, as the Scripture says: "But his flesh grieveth for him, and his soul mourneth over him" [Job 14:22].

So do they all undergo suffering, until the time when *neshamah* is enabled to reach to her proper place above. Then, however, each of the two others becomes attached to its rightful place; this is because all three are one, comprising a unity, embraced in a mystical bond.

It was incumbent on the High Priest to enter the Temple with gladness, and when he stood before His presence in that holy place, all things round about were bound to express gladness. So it is written: "Serve the Lord with gladness; come before His presence with singing" [Ps. 100:2]. This is so for the reason that in the service of the Lord, there is no place for a dejected heart.

One may ask, If a man be deeply troubled and sunk into sorrow, and his heart is heavy, yet because of tribulation he feels the urge to go to the heavenly King to seek solace; is he then to desist from praying because of his sorrowfulness? What shall he do, since he cannot help it that his heart is heavy?

The answer is that "from the day of the destruction of the Temple, all gates to heaven have been closed, but the gates of tears have not been closed,"* and suffering and sadness are expressed in tears. Standing over the gates of tears are certain heavenly beings, and they break down the bars and locks of iron, and allow the tears to enter, so that the entreaties of the grieving supplicants go through and reach the holy King, and the place of the Divine Presence is grieved by the sorrow of him who prays, as it stands written: "In all their afflictions He is afflicted" [Isa. 63:9]. . . .

And when the King, entering the place of the Presence, finds her grieving, then all her desires are granted to her.

* Talmud, Berakhot 32b.

Hence the supplication of him who sorrows does not revert empty to him, but the Holy One, be blessed, has pity on him. Blessed is the man who sheds tears as he prays before the Holy One, be blessed.

THE STARS

Once Rabbi Eleazar and Rabbi Abba were sitting together, and then the dusk came, whereupon they got up and started toward a garden by the Lake of Tiberias. Going, they beheld two stars speed toward each other from different points of the sky, meet, and then vanish.

Rabbi Abba observed: In heaven above and on the earth below, how great are the works of the Holy One, be blessed. Who fathoms it, how these two stars come from different points, how they meet and disappear?

Rabbi Eleazar answered: Nor did we need to see these two stars to reflect on them, for we have pondered on them, as we have on the multitude of great works that the Holy One, be blessed, is ever doing.

Then, quoting the verse, "Great is our Lord, and mighty in power; His understanding is without number"* [Ps. 147:5], he went on to discourse: In truth, great and mighty and sublime is the Holy One, be blessed. But, since we always knew that the Holy One, be blessed, is great and his power infinite, what new homage does David

* I.e., infinite.

show to God in these words?

Remark, nevertheless, that elsewhere in the Psalms, he says, "Great is YHVH" [Ps. 145:3], while here he says, "great is our Lord" [*adonenu*]. What is the reason? This: that when he says "Great is YHVH, and highly to be praised" [Ps. 145:3], he alludes to the higher grade, whereas here he refers to a lower grade; "great is our Lord," this corresponding to "the Lord [*adon*] of all the earth" [Josh. 3:13]. What does the verse preceding say? "He counteth the number of the stars; he giveth them all their names" [Ps. 147:4]. Were all men, since the first man, to assemble and try to count the stars, they could not succeed in reckoning them, as it stands written: "Look now toward heaven, and count the stars, if thou be able to count them" [Gen. 15:5]. While concerning the Holy One, be blessed, it says: "He counteth the number of the stars; he giveth them all their names." Why is it so? For this reason: "Great is our Lord, and mighty in power; His understanding is without number." As the stars are without number save to him, so is his understanding "without number."

Observe this also. It stands written: "He that bringeth out their host by numbers, He calleth them all by name" [Isa. 40:26]. The Holy One, be blessed, brings out all the hosts, camps and stars, and each is called by its very name, and "not one faileth" [*ibid.*]. Appointed over all these stars and constellations of the heavens are heads and leaders and ministers and it behooves them to give service to the world, each in accordance with his designated function. Nor does the smallest blade of grass in the earth fail to have its specially appointed star in heaven. And also, every star has a designated being over it, to represent it according to due rank, in ministrations before the Holy One, be blessed.

Acting as guardians over this world are all the stars of the firmaments, with each individual object of the world having a specially designated star to care for it. The herbs and the trees, the grass and the wild plants, to bloom and increase must have the power of the stars that stand over them and look directly at them, each in its particular mode. The great number of the planets and stars of all kinds emerge at the beginning of the night and shine until three hours minus a quarter after midnight. Thereafter only a small number are out. It is not without purpose that all the stars shine and serve. Some, being at their duty the whole night through, cause the plant which is their special ward to spring up and flourish. Others begin their activities at the advent of night and watch over their own object until the hour of midnight. Still others, when they have emerged and stood in conjunction with the special plant that they influence, thus speedily complete their special duty each night. So it was with the stars which we saw, which appeared briefly for their set task. When their task is accomplished, such stars vanish from this world, ascending to their allotted places above.

The book of the higher wisdom of the East tells of stars with trailing tails, comets, which from the skies hold sway over and direct the growth of certain herbs on earth, of the sort known as "elixirs of life," and influence also the growth of precious stones and gold to be found under shallow water, within the bosom of high mountains; and the growth of these is brought about by the flash of that luminous tail trailing after these stars across the firmament.

So, too, there are human ailments, as for example jaundice, which can be healed if gleaming steel is flashed rapidly back and forth before the gaze of the sufferer, thus, like a comet's tail, shooting beams of light into his face; and this brings about the cure. And it is true that without the comet's light actually passing over the things which are under the influence of such stars, these things cannot duly flourish and grow, for through the light of the comet it becomes possible for them to renew their color and reinvigorate themselves as they need. That this is true is likewise shown in the book of King Solomon, which, dealing with the science of precious stones, asserts that certain such stones are stunted in their development, never attaining their most perfect completion, if the light and dazzle of certain stars are withheld from them.

The Holy One, be blessed, has so ordered all things as to make the world perfect and full of splendor and it is therefore written that the stars are "to give light upon earth" [Gen. 1:17], upon all things necessary to the world's perfection.

The story of Jonah may be construed as an allegory of the course of a man's life in this world. Jonah descends into the ship: this is parallel to man's soul descending to enter into his body in this world. Why is the soul called Jonah [lit., aggrieved]? For the reason that she becomes subject to all manner of vexation when once she enters into partnership with the body. Thus, a man in this world is as in a ship crossing the vast ocean and like to be broken, as it is written, "so that the ship was like to be broken" [Jonah 1:4].

And then too, man in this world commits transgressions, for he supposes the Master to be disregarding the world and his presence able to be eluded. Thereupon the Almighty stirs up a raging storm; that is, the judgment of a man, which stands always before the Holy One, be blessed, and relentlessly seeks his punishment. This it is then that strikes at the ship, and remembering man's sins, seizes him; then the man is caught in the tempest and illness fells him, just as Jonah "was gone down into the innermost parts of the ship; and he lay, and was fast asleep" [ibid. 1:5]. Though the man thus lies felled, still his soul makes no move to return to his Master, to return and atone for his sins. Hence "the shipmaster came to him," that is, he who is the all-around helmsman, and the Good Inclination, "and said unto him: What meanest thou that thou sleepest? arise, call upon thy God" [ibid. 1:6]; this is no time for sleeping: you are about to be taken up to stand trial for all your deeds in this world.

Repent of your wrongdoing. Bend your mind to these matters and return to your Master.

"What is thine occupation," that is, in which you are engaged in this world, and confess now in relation to it before the Master; "and whence comest thou"; namely, from a rank droplet, and therefore refrain from arrogance before Him. "What is thy country"—consider how you came from the dust and to dust will return; "and of what people art thou" [*ibid.* 1:8]; that is, consider if you are able to place hope on being protected by virtue of your ancestors' merits.

When he is brought before the heavenly tribunal to be judged, the tempest, which was in reality the doom of judgment as it lashed out at him, calls upon the King to punish all the King's prisoners. Then the King's counsellors come before him in turn, and the tribunal is constituted. Some plead for the accused, others against him. If the man be found guilty, as with Jonah, then "the men rowed hard to bring it to the land; but they could not"; thus, they who plead for him present arguments in his favor and seek to return him to this world, but in this they fail; "for the sea grew more and more tempestuous against them" [*ibid.* 1:13]; that is, the prosecution is roused to fury against him, overwhelms the defense, and the man stands convicted of his transgressions. Thereupon three picked emissaries descend upon him. One of them draws up a balance of all the man's good deeds and all his misdeeds in this world; one takes the tally of his days; the third is he who has been constantly with the man, from the period when he was enclosed in his mother's womb.

As has been said, the judgment doom is calmed only when "they took up Jonah" [*ibid.* 1:5], when they convey the man from his home to the burial ground. Then a proclamation is sent forth concerning him, saying, if he had lived a righteous life: Honor to the image of the King! "He entereth into peace, they rest in their beds, each one that walketh in his uprightness" [Isa. 57:2]. But for a wicked man when he dies, it is proclaimed: Woe to this man, better for him had he never been born! Concerning this sort of man, it stands written, "and they cast him forth into the sea; and the sea ceased from its raging" [Jonah 1:15], which means, the doom of judgment will halt in its raging only when they have finally lowered him into the grave, which is the place of judgment. And, in truth, the fish that swallowed Jonah is the grave; and "Jonah was in the belly of the fish" [*ibid.* 2:1], which is identified with the "belly of the netherworld," as we see by the passage, "Out of the belly of the netherworld cried I" [*ibid.* 2:3].

"Three days and three nights" [*ibid.* 2:1]: which means the three days that a man is in his grave before his belly bursts apart. At the end of three days, it casts forth its putrescence onto his face, saying: Receive back that which you put into me; all day long you ate and drank, nor ever gave a thing to the poor; like feasts and holidays were all your days, but the needy did not share your food and were left hungry. Receive back that which you put into me. . . .

And, three days more having elapsed, the man is punished in each organ, in his eyes, his hands, his feet. For thirty days, then, the soul and the body receive punishment together. Therefore does the soul tarry during this time on earth below, and does not ascend to her sphere, as a woman is isolated through the period of her impurity.

Then the soul does ascend, and the body continues to molder in the earth, and there will lie until the hour when the Holy One, be blessed, shall rouse up the dead. At that time a voice will be heard ringing through the graves, and proclaiming: "Awake and sing, ye that dwell in the dust —for Thy dew is as the dew of light, and the earth shall bring to life the shades" [*refaim;* Isa. 26:19]. This will be when the Angel of Death shall vanish from the world, as it stands written: "He will swallow up death for ever; and the Lord God will wipe away tears from off all faces; and the reproach of his people will He take away from off all the earth" [*ibid.* 25:8].

It is that event which is alluded to in the words: "And the Lord spoke unto the fish, and it vomited out Jonah upon the dry land" [Jonah 2:11]; when the graves hear the trumpeting of that voice, they will promptly eject the dead bodies that lie in them. And the dead will assume their pristine bodily condition, as is indicated by the word *refaim* [shades] which is related to *rafah* [healing]. . . .

So we see that the story of that fish holds words of solace for the entire world. No sooner had it swallowed Jonah than it died, yet three days later it was restored to life, and vomited him forth. And in like manner, in the future, the land of Israel will be roused first to new life, and then "the earth shall bring to life the shades."

LEVITICUS
NUMBERS
DEUTERONOMY

Once, as Rabbi Aha and Rabbi Judah were walking along together, Rabbi Judah said: We have learned that the virgin of Israel* is blessed sevenfold, yet the Scripture says concerning her, "And do thou, O son of man, take up a lamentation for the virgin of Israel";† and still worse, "The virgin of Israel is fallen, she shall no more rise" [Amos 5:2]. This latter verse has, indeed, been interpreted by all the Companions to be a message of comfort.‡ But that is not probable; the prophet himself refers to it as a lamentation.

To this answered Rabbi Aha: The same difficulty has vexed me as well. I came before Rabbi Simeon, and I looked to be greatly harassed.

He remarked: Your face reveals that something troubles your mind.

Said I: In truth, my mind is as downcast as my face is.

He asked me: What is it then?

I spoke: It is written, "The virgin of Israel is fallen, she shall no more rise." If a man's wife leaves him because of his anger with her, shall she not ever return? Then, alas

---

* The Divine Presence as the mystical embodiment of the Community of Israel.

† This verse, not found in our Scriptures, is apparently a paraphrase of Ezek. 19:1, "Moreover take thou up a lamentation for the princes of Israel."

‡ In the Talmud, Berakhot 4b, the verse is interpreted thus: "She has fallen, but shall no more; rise, O virgin of Israel."

for the children who must go with her!

He answered me: Is not what the Companions have said explanation enough?

I answered: I have heard what they say, that it is a message of comfort, but it does not content me.

He said: The Companions' explanation is correct in what it says, but more is to be said. Woe to the generation lacking in shepherds, when the sheep stray, knowing no direction. This verse does in truth need understanding, yet is altogether clear to whoever can interpret the Torah properly. Come and see. All the other exiles of Israel had a set period, and when this term ended, Israel returned to God, the virgin of Israel returned to her place. But this last exile is different, and she shall not return as heretofore, which is indicated by the verse, "The virgin of Israel is fallen, she shall no more rise." See that it is not written, "I shall not raise her any more."

Think of a king who in anger against his queen banished her from his palace for a stated time. That time elapsed, she forthwith returned to the king. Thus did it come to pass several times. Then, however, came a time when she was banished from the palace of the king for a lengthy period. The king said: Now it is not like before, when she returned to me. Now, this time, I shall go, taking all my followers, to seek her out. And when he found her, she was in the dust. Seeing her thus trampled, and yearning anew for her, the king took her by the hand and raised her up, and led her back to the palace, and promised on his oath he would never again send her away.

So with the Community of Israel: whenever previously she was in exile, at the appointed time, she was wont of herself to return to the King; now, in this exile, the Holy One, be blessed, will go and take her by the hand and raise her, and give her comfort, and bring her back to his palace. Thus it is written: "In that day will I raise up the tabernacle of David that is fallen" [Amos 9:11]; and the "tabernacle of David" is the same as the virgin of Israel.

Said Rabbi Judah: You have indeed comforted and contented me, and this is the true conception. It puts me in mind of a similar idea which I had forgotten, a thing that Rabbi Yose said, that the Holy One, be blessed, will in a future day proclaim in regard to the Community of Israel, and say: "Shake thyself from the dust; arise, and sit down, O Jerusalem" [Isa. 52:2], as a man takes the hand of his neighbor and says, Come now, compose yourself.

Rabbi Aha then said to him: The same kind of speech is used by all the prophets. Thus is it written, "Arise, shine, for thy light is come" [Isa. 60:1], and it means that the King is at hand to offer reconciliation to her. And also, "Behold thy king cometh unto thee" [Zech. 9:9]; and it signifies, He shall come to you to raise you and comfort you, to make all up to you, to bring you into his palace and to espouse you for always, as it is written: "And I will betroth thee unto Me for ever" [Hos. 2:21].

Discoursing on the text: "Serve the Lord with joy, come before His presence with singing" [Ps. 100:2], Rabbi Judah said: We have learned that the service of God which is not made with joy and zeal, that service is imperfect. But what if a man sins against the commands of the law, and then in repentance goes to offer service to God? Of what countenance can a man be on such occasion, standing before the Lord? Verily, he is then grieved of heart and penitent of spirit, and how then shall he show joy and singing? The truth is, however, that the priests and Levites did it; it was the priest who performed the rejoicing, because he is far from chastisement, and is bound ever to manifest a joyful countenance, more so than the others. And as for the singing, this the Levites performed, whose function it was. Thus the priest was stationed by the man and with fitting words he unified the holy Name in joy, and at the same time the Levites performed the singing.

But in these days of no offerings, how is that man to manifest joy and singing who returns to his Master heavy-hearted and sorrowful, in tears and repentance? The answer is based on a secret. We have learned: A man should go into the synagogue to the distance of two gateways and then pray. This is a reference to the words of David: "Lift up your heads, O ye gates" [Ps. 24:7]. These gates are two grades, and they are found far within; they are the grades Mercy [hesed] and Fear [pahad], at their commencement, and they are the gateways of the [inner] world. Hence in prayer a man must needs fix his thoughts on the Holy of Holies, that is, the holy Name, and then utter his prayer.

The same lesson is also learned in this: Joy is a secret name of the Community of Israel, and there will come a day when Israel shall go out of the exile by means of joy, as it is written, "For ye shall go out with joy" [Isa. 55:12], and hence it says, "Serve the Lord with joy." It says also, "Come before His presence with singing." Thus is the joy made complete, for the heart holds the joy and the mouth holds the song.

So we see that this is the meet way for a man to appear before his Master, for then it may be said to him, "Know ye that the Lord He is God" [Ps. 100:3]; it rests with him then to unify the holy Name, make these two names one by conjoining them, and in this is the true service of the Holy One, be blessed.

HYMNS IN HEAVEN

"And he shall go out unto the altar that is before the Lord" [Lev. 16:18]. In this connection Rabbi Judah quoted the verse: "God, God, the Lord, hath spoken, and called the earth from the rising of the sun unto the going down thereof" [Ps. 50:1].

He said: It has been taught us that at the break of the day a chorus of a thousand and five hundred and fifty myriads sing out hymns to God, and at midday, a thousand

and five hundred and forty-eight, and at the time which is known as "between the evenings," a thousand and five hundred and ninety myriads.

Rabbi Yose commented that at the dawning of the day all the heavenly hosts which are known as the "lords of shouting" greet it with utterances of praise, for then are all jubilant, and then judgment is lightened. At this moment the world rejoices and is blessed, and the Holy One, be blessed, rouses up Abraham [the representative of Mercy], and holds glad converse with him and allows him the sway over the world. But at the time known as "between the evenings" the angels called "masters of howling" raise their voices, and through the world, contentiousness prevails. Then the Holy One, be blessed, bidding Isaac [the representative of stern Judgment], rise up, moves to judge the transgressors of the precepts of the law. There come forth seven rivers of fire to descend on the heads of the wicked, and also the burning coals of fire. Now Abraham retreats back, the day departs, and in Gehinnom the evildoers, groaning, cry: "Woe unto us! for the day declineth, for the shadows of the evening are stretched out" [Jer. 6:4].

Thus, at this hour, a man should take heed not to overlook the afternoon prayer. With the arrival of night, there are called forth from outside the curtain the other fifteen hundred and forty-eight myriads, and they intone hymns, whereupon the punishments from the netherworld are roused up and wander about the world, chanting praises until midnight, which is a watch and a half. Then, the north wind having stirred up and gone out, all the remaining congregate to sing Psalms until the daylight breaks and the morning stirs up, and gladness and blessing come back to the world.

HOLY COMMUNION

Rabbi Abba cited the verse: "And who is like Thy people, like Israel, a nation one in the earth?" [II Sam. 7:3]. Said he: God chose Israel and none other from among the peoples and established them in the world as a single unique nation and, after his own name, he called them "one nation." To crown them, he bestowed upon them a multitude of precepts, and with these the phylacteries of the head and the arm, which makes a man one and complete. It is only when he is complete that a man is called "one," but not if he is lacking, and so God when he is made complete with the patriarchs and the Community of Israel, then is he called One.

In this wise, donning his phylacteries and enfolding himself in the prayer shawl, the Israelite is crowned with holy crowns in the heavenly manner, and is called "one." Then it is proper that One should come and give heed to one.

When is "one" said of a man? When he is male together with female and is highly sanctified and zealous for sanctification; then and only then he is designated one without mar of any kind. Hence a man and his wife should have a single inclination at the hour of their union, and the man should be glad with his wife, attaching her to himself in affection. So conjoined, they make one soul and one body: a single soul through their affection; a single body, for only when male and female are conjoined do they form a single body; whereas, and this we have learned, if a man is not wedded, he is, we may say, divided in two. But when male and female are joined, God abides upon "one" and endows it with a holy spirit; and, as was said, these are called the children of the Holy One, be blessed.

GOD'S LOVE

Rabbi Abba considered the verse: "O turn unto me, and be gracious unto me; give Thy strength unto Thy servant" [Ps. 86:16].

He said: Does it mean David was the most beautiful that God could turn to? The meaning is that God, as we have learned, possesses another David, one who commands numbers of heavenly hosts and legions; and, desiring to bestow his grace upon the world, God directs a smiling countenance upon this "David" [the Divine Presence], who then, by virtue of his beauty, illuminates the world and engraces it. His head is a golden skull embellished with seven gold ornaments. God loves him greatly, and so instructs him to turn and gaze at him with his surpassingly fair eyes, which, when he does, causes God's heart, so to speak, to be pierced with shafts of celestial affection. It was for the sake of that heavenly and comely David, the object of God's love and desire, that David said: "O turn unto me, and be gracious unto me."

So it was when Isaac said to Jacob, "See, the smell of my son is as the smell of a field which the Lord hath blessed" [Gen. 27:27]. We have been taught that this was so because accompanying Jacob when he went in was the Garden of Eden. We may ask, again: how could the Garden of Eden enter with him, stretching as it does an immense length and breadth, and with numerous sections and abodes? In reality, God possesses another holy garden. He has a special affection for it, and watches over it himself, and he charges it to accompany the righteous always. This garden it was that entered with Jacob.

Likewise, when the story is told that the entire land of Israel came and put itself under Abram,* it signifies another land which God has, a holy and celestial land which is known also as "the land of Israel." This land of Israel lies beneath the mystical abode of Jacob, and God, out of his love for them, has given it to Israel to be with them and lead them and stand guard over them; it is known as "the land of the living."

*According to a midrash on Gen. 13:15.

Discoursing on the verse: "I am a rose of Sharon, a lily of the valleys" [Cant. 2:1], Rabbi Simeon said: The Holy One, be blessed, bears great love to the Community of Israel, wherefore he constantly praises her, and she, from the store of chants and hymns she keeps for the King, constantly sings his praises.

Because she flowers splendidly in the Garden of Eden, the Community of Israel is called rose of Sharon; because her desire is to be watered from the deep stream which is the source of all spiritual rivers, she is called lily of the valleys.

Also, because she is found at the deepest place is she designated lily of the valleys. At first, she is a rose with yellowish petals, and then a lily of two colors, white and red, a lily of six petals, changing from one hue to another. She is named "rose" when she is about to join with the King, and after she has come together with him in her kisses, she is named "lily."

Remark this: that God, when he made man and clothed him in great honor, made it incumbent that he cleave to him so as to be unique and of single heart, united to the One by the tie of the single-purposed faith which ties all together. But later, men abandoned the road of faith and left behind the singular tree which looms high over all trees, and adhered to the place which is continually shifting from one hue to another, from good to evil and evil to good, and they descended from on high and adhered below to the uncertain, and deserted the supreme and changeless One. Thus it was that their hearts, shifting between good and evil, caused them at times to merit mercy, at others punishment, depending on what it was that they had cleaved to.

The Holy One, be blessed, spoke: Man, life you have abandoned, and to death you cleave; truly, death awaits you.—And so the decree was death, for him and for all the world.

But if Adam transgressed, in what did the rest of the world sin? We know that all creatures did not come and eat of the forbidden tree, no. But it was this way: when man stood upright, all creatures, beholding him, were seized with fear of him, and slavelike they followed after him. And hence when he addressed them: Come, let us bow down to the Lord who did make us—they followed suit. But when they observed him making obeisance to the other place, adhering to it, again, they did the same, and in this wise did he bring about death for himself and all the world.

So did Adam move back and forth from one hue to another, from good to evil, from evil to good, from agitation to rest, from judgment to mercy, from life to death: never consistent in any one thing, because of the effect of that place, which is thus known as "the flaming sword which turned every way" [Gen. 3:24], from this direction to that, from good to evil, from mercy to judgment, from peace to war.

But the supreme King, out of compassion for his own handiworks, gave them warning, and said: "Of the tree of the knowledge of good and evil, thou shalt not eat of it" [Gen. 2:17]. Not heeding, man did as his wife, and was banished for ever, inasmuch as woman can come to this place, but not farther, and on her account death was decreed for all. But in time to come, "the days of my people shall be as the days of the tree" [Isa. 65:22], like that singular tree we know of. Concerning that time it is written, "He will swallow up death for ever; and the Lord God will wipe away tears from all faces" [*ibid.* 25:8].

Rabbi Simeon said: If a man looks upon the Torah as merely a book presenting narratives and everyday matters, alas for him! Such a torah, one treating with everyday concerns, and indeed a more excellent one, we too, even we, could compile. More than that, in the possession of the rulers of the world there are books of even greater merit, and these we could emulate if we wished to compile some such torah. But the Torah, in all of its words, holds supernal truths and sublime secrets.

See how precisely balanced are the upper and the lower worlds. Israel here below is balanced by the angels on high, concerning whom it stands written: "who makest thy angels into winds" [Ps. 104:4]. For when the angels descend to earth they don earthly garments, else they could neither abide in the world, nor could it bear to have them. But if this is so with the angels, then how much more so it must be with the Torah: the Torah it was that created the angels and created all the worlds and through Torah are all sustained. The world could not endure the Torah if she had not garbed herself in garments of this world.

Thus the tales related in the Torah are simply her outer garments, and woe to the man who regards that outer garb as the Torah itself, for such a man will be deprived of portion in the next world. Thus David said: "Open Thou mine eyes, that I may behold wondrous things out of Thy law" [Ps. 119:18], that is to say, the things that are underneath. See now. The most visible part of a man are the clothes that he has on, and they who lack understanding, when they look at the man, are apt not to see more in him than these clothes. In reality, however, it is the body of the man that constitutes the pride of his clothes, and his soul constitutes the pride of his body.

So it is with the Torah. Its narrations which relate to things of the world constitute the garments which clothe the body of the Torah; and that body is composed of the Torah's precepts, *gufey-torah* [bodies, major principles]. People without understanding see only the narrations, the garment; those somewhat more penetrating see also the body. But the truly wise, those who serve the most high King and stood on mount Sinai, pierce all the way through to the soul, to the true Torah which is the root principle of all. These same will in the future be vouchsafed to penetrate to the very soul of the soul of the Torah.

See now how it is like this in the highest world, with garment, body, soul and super-soul. The outer garments are the heavens and all therein, the body is the Community of Israel and it is the recipient of the soul, that is "the Glory of Israel"; and the soul of the soul is the Ancient Holy One. All of these are conjoined one within the other.

Woe to the sinners who look upon the Torah as simply tales pertaining to things of the world, seeing thus only the outer garment. But the righteous whose gaze penetrates to the very Torah, happy are they. Just as wine must be in a jar to keep, so the Torah must be contained in an outer garment. That garment is made up of the tales and stories; but we, we are bound to penetrate beyond.

TEXTS

The Roman numerals and the pagination refer to the standard editions of the Zohar which in turn follow the first edition, Mantua 1558–60.

ACKNOWLEDGMENTS

The English rendition of the selected Zohar passages was prepared under the supervision of Professor Scholem, with the special assistance of Sherry Abel. The English Zohar translation of Soncino Press was consulted, and the suggestions received are gratefully acknowledged. The Bible has been quoted according to the translation of the Jewish Publication Society of America, except where the context required a different rendition. The editor's Introduction was translated by Prof. Ralph Marcus.